HUMAN BODY I

Britannica Illustrated Science Library

Encyclopædia Britannica, Inc.

Chicago ▪ London ▪ New Delhi ▪ Paris ▪ Seoul ▪ Sydney ▪ Taipei ▪ Tokyo

Britannica Illustrated Science Library

Idea and Concept of This Work: Editorial Sol 90

Project Management: Fabián Cassan

Photo Credits: Corbis, ESA, Getty Images, Graphic News, NASA, National Geographic, Science Photo Library

Illustrators: Guido Arroyo, Pablo Aschei, Carlos Francisco Bulzomi, Gustavo J. Caironi, Hernán Cañellas, Leonardo César, José Luis Corsetti, Vanina Farías, Manrique Fernández Buente, Joana Garrido, Celina Hilbert, Inkspot, Jorge Ivanovich, Iván Longuini, Isidro López, Diego Martín, Jorge Martínez, Marco Menco, Marcelo Morán, Ala de Mosca, Diego Mourelos, Laura Mourelos, Pablo Palastro, Eduardo Pérez, Javier Pérez, Ariel Piroyansky, Fernando Ramallo, Ariel Roldán, Marcel Socías, Néstor Taylor, Trebol Animation, Juan Venegas, Constanza Vicco, Coralia Vignau, Gustavo Yamin, 3DN, 3DOM studio

Composition and Pre-press Services: Editorial Sol 90
Translation Services and Index: Publication Services, Inc.

Britannica Illustrated Science Library Staff

Editorial
Michael Levy, *Executive Editor, Core Editorial*
John Rafferty, *Associate Editor, Earth Sciences*
William L. Hosch, *Associate Editor, Mathematics and Computers*
Kara Rogers, *Associate Editor, Life Sciences*
Rob Curley, *Senior Editor, Science and Technology*
David Hayes, *Special Projects Editor*

Art and Composition
Steven N. Kapusta, *Director*
Carol A. Gaines, *Composition Supervisor*
Christine McCabe, *Senior Illustrator*

Media Acquisition
Kathy Nakamura, *Manager*

Copy Department
Sylvia Wallace, *Director*
Julian Ronning, *Supervisor*

Information Management and Retrieval
Sheila Vasich, *Information Architect*

Production Control
Marilyn L. Barton

Manufacturing
Kim Gerber, *Director*

Encyclopædia Britannica, Inc.

Jacob E. Safra, *Chairman of the Board*

Jorge Aguilar-Cauz, *President*

Michael Ross, *Senior Vice President, Corporate Development*

Dale H. Hoiberg, *Senior Vice President and Editor*

Marsha Mackenzie, *Director of Production*

International Standard Book Number (set):
 978-1-59339-382-3
International Standard Book Number (volume):
 978-1-59339-390-8
Britannica Illustrated Science Library: Human Body I 2008

Printed in China

ENCYCLOPÆDIA
Britannica®

www.britannica.com

Human Body I

Contents

What Are We Made Of?

Page 6

Bones and Muscles

Page 18

Internal Systems and Organs

Page 34

The Senses and Speech

Page 68

Control Centers

Page 80

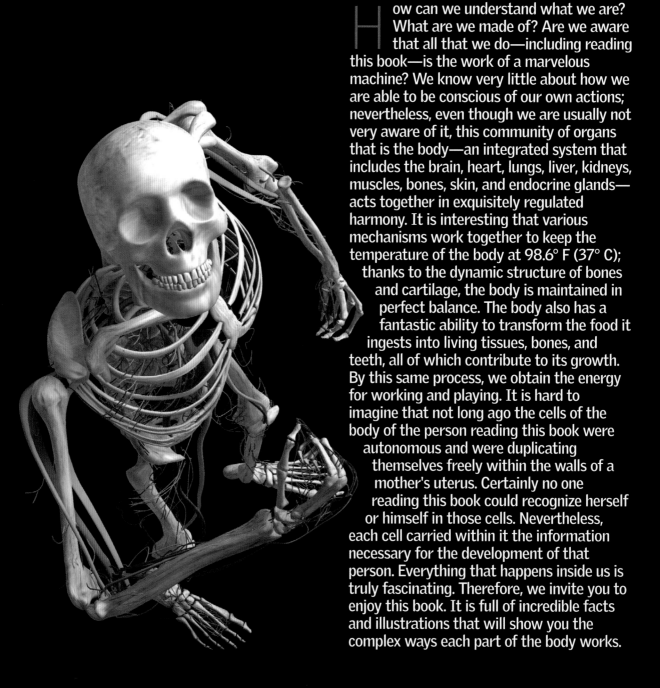

A LIVING STRUCTURE
The skeleton consists of 206 separate bones, which differ in form, size, and name. It supports and shapes the body, protects the internal organs, and—in the bone marrow of certain bones—manufactures various types of blood cells.

A Perfect Machine

How can we understand what we are? What are we made of? Are we aware that all that we do—including reading this book—is the work of a marvelous machine? We know very little about how we are able to be conscious of our own actions; nevertheless, even though we are usually not very aware of it, this community of organs that is the body—an integrated system that includes the brain, heart, lungs, liver, kidneys, muscles, bones, skin, and endocrine glands— acts together in exquisitely regulated harmony. It is interesting that various mechanisms work together to keep the temperature of the body at 98.6° F (37° C); thanks to the dynamic structure of bones and cartilage, the body is maintained in perfect balance. The body also has a fantastic ability to transform the food it ingests into living tissues, bones, and teeth, all of which contribute to its growth. By this same process, we obtain the energy for working and playing. It is hard to imagine that not long ago the cells of the body of the person reading this book were autonomous and were duplicating themselves freely within the walls of a mother's uterus. Certainly no one reading this book could recognize herself or himself in those cells. Nevertheless, each cell carried within it the information necessary for the development of that person. Everything that happens inside us is truly fascinating. Therefore, we invite you to enjoy this book. It is full of incredible facts and illustrations that will show you the complex ways each part of the body works.

What are cells like, and how do they form tissue? What is blood, and why are proteins so important? The heart, usually thought of as the wellspring of love and the emotions, is actually the engine of the circulatory system. It is because of the heart that all the cells of the body receive a constant supply of nutrients, oxygen, and other essential substances. The heart is so powerful that it pumps about 10 pints (4.7 l) of blood per minute. The nervous system is the most intricate of all the body's systems. It works every second of every day, gathering information about the organism and its surroundings and issuing instructions so that the organism can react. It is this computer that permits us to think and remember and that makes us who we are.

The nervous system is a complex network of sensory cells, originating in the brain and spinal cord, that transmits signals throughout the body, employing a caravan of chemical messengers to make sense of this marvelous complex that we catalogue as touch, taste, smell, hearing, and vision. In fact, at this precise moment, because of an extraordinary relationship between our eyes and our brain, we are able to see and understand what we are reading. Modern cameras are designed on the same basic principles as our eye, but they have never been able to equal the visual power of the eye. The focus and the automatic aperture of the human eye are perfect. Our ears share a similar complexity and allow us to have excellent hearing. The external ear operates by receiving sound waves in the air. Sound waves travel through the auditory canal and are transmitted by the bones of the intermediate ear toward the cochlea, which contains liquid and is spiraled like the shell of a small sea snail. The cochlea converts waves of air into vibrations of liquid, which are detected by special filaments in the ear that are of many lengths and that detect sound waves of different lengths. These filaments then transmit nerve impulses to the brain and provide us with our ability to interpret what we hear. This book will also tell you about the function of our skin, the largest organ of the body, which serves as an elastic barrier covering and protecting everything inside our bodies. Captivating images will show you how each of our extraordinary body systems function, and incredible facts will help you understand why the human body is so amazing. ●

What Are We Made Of?

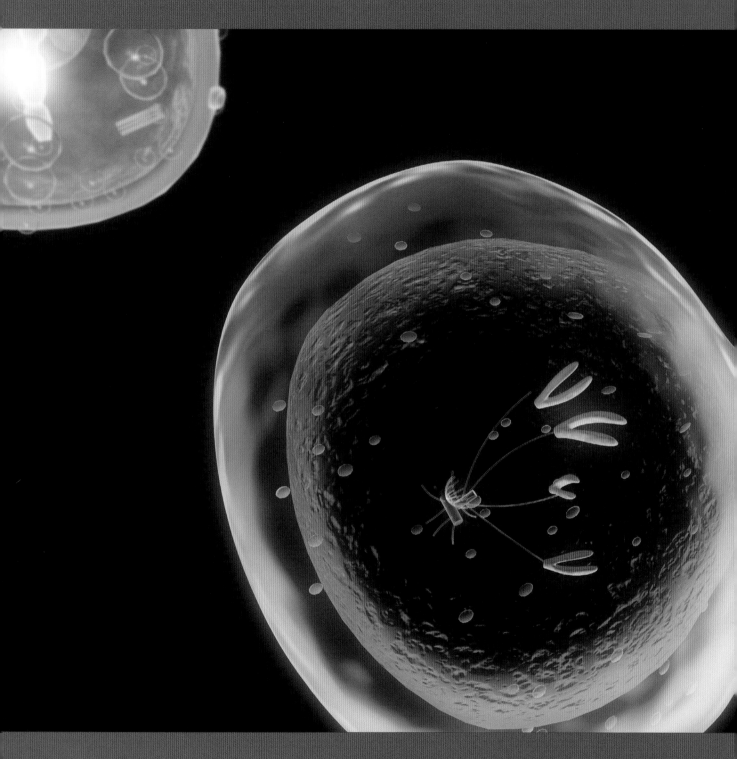

To understand the truest and most elementary characteristics of life, we must begin with the cell-the tiny organizing structure of life in all its forms.

Most cells are too small to be observed with the naked eye, but they can be distinguished easily through an ordinary microscope. Human body tissues are groups of cells whose size

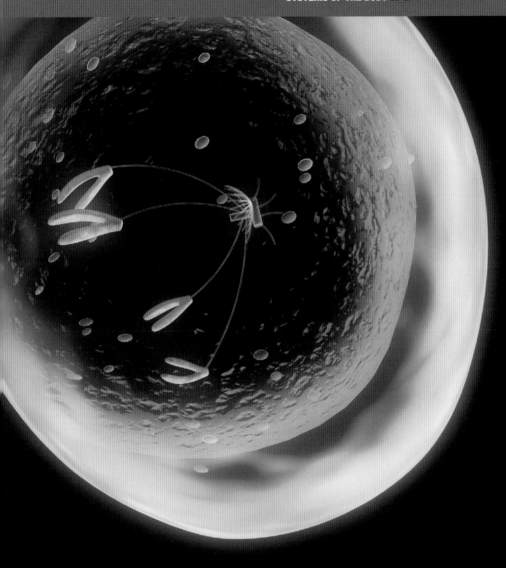

MITOSIS
An enlarged view that shows
the process of mitosis, the
most common form of
cellular division

UNDIVIDED ATTENTION 8-9

WATER AND LIQUIDS 10-11

THE CELL 12-13

MITOSIS 14-15

SYSTEMS OF THE BODY 16-17

and shape depend on the specific tissue to which they belong. Did you know that an embryo is a mass of rapidly dividing cells that continue to develop during infancy? We invite you to turn the page and discover many surprising things in this fascinating and complex world. ●

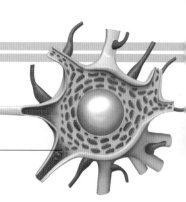

Neurons

Each neuron in the brain can be connected with several thousand other neurons and is capable of receiving 100,000 signals per second. The signals travel through the nervous system at a speed of 225 miles per hour (360 km/h). Thanks to this complex communication network, the brain is capable of remembering, calculating, deciding, and thinking.

DENDRITES
They are the branches through which a neuron receives and sends messages. With this system each neuron can be stimulated by thousands of other neurons, which in turn can stimulate other neurons, and so forth.

Undivided Attention

From birth the infant's brain cells develop rapidly, making connections that can shape all of life's experiences. The first three years are crucial. When neurons receive visual, auditory, or gustatory stimuli, they send messages that generate new physical connections with neighboring cells. The signals are sent through a gap called a synapse by means of a complex electrochemical process. What determines the formation of a person's synapses and neural networks? One key factor is believed to be the undivided attention and mental effort exerted by the person.

Learning

Each child has his or her own intellectual filter; the quality of the filter depends on undivided attention and on how the child responds to a broad variety of stimuli.

225 miles per hour
(360 km/h)
THE VELOCITY OF THE NERVOUS
SYSTEM'S SIGNALS

Brain

At birth the infant brain contains 100 billion neurons. That is about as many nerve cells as there are stars in the entire Milky Way Galaxy! Then as the infant receives messages from the senses, the cerebral cortex begins its dynamic development.

3 pounds
(1.4 kg)
IS THE WEIGHT OF
A HUMAN BRAIN.

Respiration

Respiration is usually an involuntary, automatic action that allows us to take in the oxygen we need from the air and exhale carbon dioxide. These gases are exchanged in the pulmonary alveoli.

A WORLD OF SENSATIONS
The tongue recognizes four tastes (sweet, salty, sour, and bitter), and the nasal fossas contain cells that have more than 200 million filaments, called cilia, which are capable of detecting thousands of odors.

THE SENSE OF TOUCH
It is predominant in the fingers and hands. The information is transmitted through neurotransmitters, nerves that carry these impulses to the brain and that serve to detect sensations such as cold, heat, pressure, and pain.

SKIN
The skin is one of the most important organs of the body. It contains approximately five million tiny nerve endings that transmit sensations.

Water and Fluids

Water is of such great importance that it makes up almost two thirds of the human body by weight. Water is present in all the tissues of the body. It plays a fundamental role in digestion and absorption and in the elimination of indigestible metabolic waste. Water also serves as the basis of the circulatory system, which uses blood to distribute nutrients to the entire body. Moreover, water helps maintain body temperature by expelling excess heat through the skin via perspiration and evaporation. Perspiration and evaporation of water account for most of the weight a person loses while exercising. ●

Water Balance and Food

In its continuous process of taking in and eliminating water, one of the most important functions of the body is to maintain a continuous equilibrium between the water that enters and the water that leaves the body. Because the body does not have an organ or other place for storing water, quantities that are lost must be continuously replenished. The human body can survive for several weeks without taking in food, but going without water for the same length of time would have tragic consequences. The human being takes in about 2.5 to 3 quarts (2.5-3 l) of water per day. About half is taken in by drinking, and the rest comes from eating solid food. Some foods, such as fruits and vegetables, consist of 95 percent water. Eggs are 90 percent water, and red meat and fish are 60 to 70 percent water.

60%

THE PERCENTAGE OF A PERSON'S WEIGHT THAT IS DUE TO WATER. IN GENERAL, A 10 PERCENT LOSS OF WATER LEADS TO SERIOUS DISORDERS, AND A LOSS OF 20 PERCENT RESULTS IN DEATH.

HOW THIRST IS CONTROLLED
Thirst is the sensation through which the nervous system informs its major organ, the brain, that the body needs water. The control center is the hypothalamus. If the concentration of plasma in the blood increases, it means the body is losing water. Dry mouth and a lack of saliva are also indications that the body needs water.

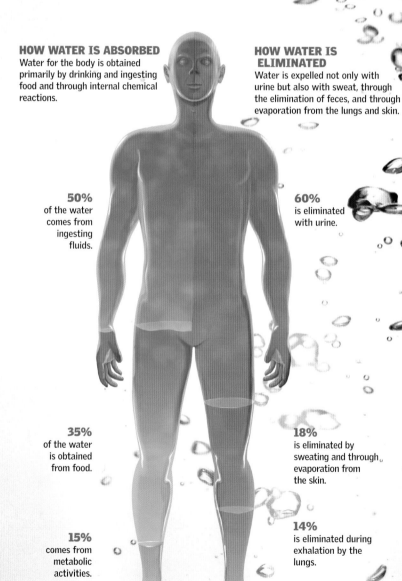

HOW WATER IS ABSORBED
Water for the body is obtained primarily by drinking and ingesting food and through internal chemical reactions.

HOW WATER IS ELIMINATED
Water is expelled not only with urine but also with sweat, through the elimination of feces, and through evaporation from the lungs and skin.

50%
of the water comes from ingesting fluids.

35%
of the water is obtained from food.

15%
comes from metabolic activities.

60%
is eliminated with urine.

18%
is eliminated by sweating and through evaporation from the skin.

14%
is eliminated during exhalation by the lungs.

8%
is eliminated in excrement.

Chemical Elements

The body contains many chemical elements. The most common are oxygen, hydrogen, carbon, and nitrogen, which are found mainly in proteins. Nine chemical elements are present in moderate amounts, and the rest (such as zinc) are present only in very small amounts, so they are called trace elements.

0.004% IRON
Fluids and tissues, bones, proteins. An iron deficiency causes anemia, whose symptoms include fatigue and paleness. Iron is essential for the formation of hemoglobin in the blood.

 MAGNESIUM 0.05%
Lungs, kidneys, liver, thyroid, brain, muscles, heart

 CALCIUM 1.5%
Bones, lungs, kidneys, liver, thyroid, brain, muscles, heart

 SODIUM 0.15%
Fluids and tissues, in the form of salt

 CHLORINE 0.2%
maintains the equilibrium of water in the blood.

POTASSIUM 0.3%
Nerves and muscles; inside the cell

PHOSPHORUS 1%
Urine, bones

0.0004% IODINE
Urine, bones. When consumed, iodine passes into the blood and from there into the thyroid gland. Among its other functions, iodine is used by the thyroid to produce growth hormones for most of the organs and for brain development.

 SULFUR 0.3%
Contained in numerous proteins, especially in the contractile proteins

C **18% CARBON**
Present in all organic molecules

Proteins
Proteins are formed through the combination of the four most common chemical elements found in the body. Proteins include insulin, which is secreted by the pancreas to regulate the amount of sugar in the blood.

H **10% HYDROGEN**
Present in water, nutrients, and organic molecules

N **3% NITROGEN**
Present in proteins and nucleic acids

O **65% OXYGEN**
Present in water and in almost all organic molecules

The Cell

It is the smallest unit of the human body—and of all living organisms—able to function autonomously. It is so small that it can be seen only with a microscope. Its essential parts are the nucleus and cytoplasm, which are surrounded by a membrane. Each cell reproduces independently through a process called mitosis. The animal kingdom does have single-celled organisms, but in a body such as that of a human being millions of cells are organized into tissues and organs. The word "cell" comes from Latin; it is the diminutive of *cella*, which means "hollow." The science of studying cells is called cytology. ●

Cell Theory

Before the invention of the microscope, it was impossible to see cells. Some biological theories were therefore based on logical speculations rather than on observation. People believed in "spontaneous generation" because it was inconceivable that cells would regenerate. The development of the microscope, including that of an electronic version in the 20th century, made detailed observation of the internal structure of the cell possible. Robert Hooke was the first to see dead cells in 1665. In 1838 Mathias Schleiden observed living cells, and in 1839, in collaboration with Theodor Schwann, he developed the first theory of cells: that all living organisms consist of cells.

THEODOR SCHWANN

MATHIAS SCHLEIDEN

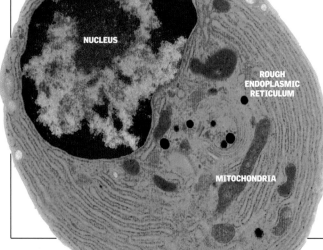

NUCLEUS

ROUGH ENDOPLASMIC RETICULUM

MITOCHONDRIA

UNDER THE MICROSCOPE

This cell has been magnified 4,000 times with an electron microscope. The nucleus is clearly visible, along with some typical organelles in the green-colored cytoplasm.

CYTOSKELETON
Composed of fibers, the cytoskeleton is responsible for cell motion, or cytokinesis.

LYSOSOME
This is the "stomach" of the cell because it breaks down waste molecules with its enzymes.

GOLGI APPARATUS
This structure processes proteins produced by the rough endoplasmatic reticulum and places them in sacs called vesicles.

ROUGH ENDOPLASMATIC RETICULUM
A labyrinthine assembly of canals and membranous spaces that transport proteins and are involved in the synthesis of substances.

RIBOSOME
This organelle is where the last stages of protein synthesis take place.

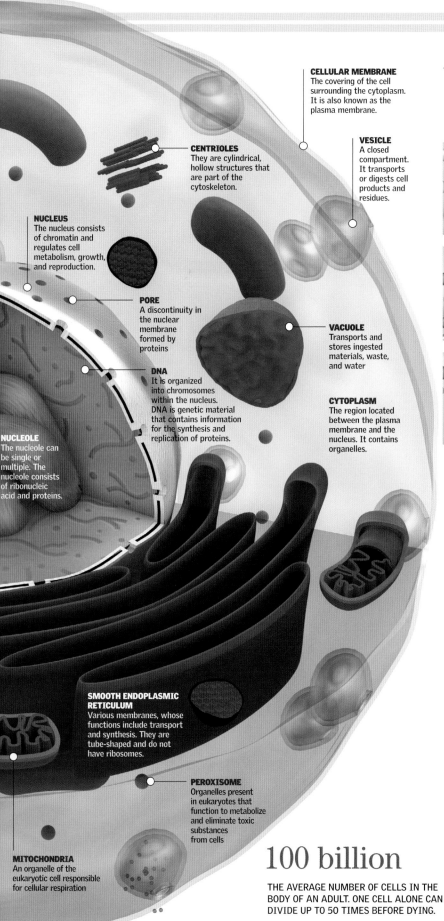

CELLULAR MEMBRANE
The covering of the cell surrounding the cytoplasm. It is also known as the plasma membrane.

CENTRIOLES
They are cylindrical, hollow structures that are part of the cytoskeleton.

VESICLE
A closed compartment. It transports or digests cell products and residues.

NUCLEUS
The nucleus consists of chromatin and regulates cell metabolism, growth, and reproduction.

PORE
A discontinuity in the nuclear membrane formed by proteins

VACUOLE
Transports and stores ingested materials, waste, and water

DNA
It is organized into chromosomes within the nucleus. DNA is genetic material that contains information for the synthesis and replication of proteins.

CYTOPLASM
The region located between the plasma membrane and the nucleus. It contains organelles.

NUCLEOLE
The nucleole can be single or multiple. The nucleole consists of ribonucleic acid and proteins.

SMOOTH ENDOPLASMIC RETICULUM
Various membranes, whose functions include transport and synthesis. They are tube-shaped and do not have ribosomes.

PEROXISOME
Organelles present in eukaryotes that function to metabolize and eliminate toxic substances from cells

MITOCHONDRIA
An organelle of the eukaryotic cell responsible for cellular respiration

100 billion

THE AVERAGE NUMBER OF CELLS IN THE BODY OF AN ADULT. ONE CELL ALONE CAN DIVIDE UP TO 50 TIMES BEFORE DYING.

TRANSPORT MECHANISMS

The cell membrane is a semipermeable barrier. The cell exchanges nutrients and waste between its cytoplasm and the extracellular medium via passive and active transport mechanisms.

DIFFUSION It is a passive transport mechanism in which the cell does not use energy. The particles that cross the cell membrane do so because of a concentration gradient. For example, water, oxygen, and carbon dioxide circulate by diffusion.

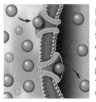

FACILITATED DIFFUSION
Passive transport in which substances, typically ions (electrically charged particles), that because of their size could not otherwise penetrate the cell's bilayer can do so through a pore consisting of proteins. Glucose enters the cell in this way.

ACTIVE TRANSPORT It occurs by means of proteins and requires energy consumption by the cell because the direction of ion transport is against the concentration gradient. In some cells, such as neurons, the Na+/K+ pump uses active transport to move ions into or out of the cell.

Mitochondria

The mitochondria provide large amounts of energy to the cell. They contain a variety of enzymes that, together with oxygen, degrade products derived from glycolysis and carry out cellular respiration. The amount of energy obtained in this process is almost 20 times as great as that released by glycolysis in the cytoplasm. Mitochondria are very different from other organelles because they have a unique structure: an external membrane enclosing an internal membrane with a great number of folds that delimit the internal area, or mitochondrial matrix. In addition, the mitochondria have a circular chromosome similar to that of bacteria that allows the mitochondria to replicate. Cells that need a relatively large amount of energy have many mitochondria because the cells reproduce frequently.

Mitosis

I t is the cell-division process that results in the formation of cells that are genetically identical to the original (or mother) cell and to each other. The copies arise through replication and division of the chromosomes, or genetic material, in such a way that each of the daughter cells receives a similar inheritance of chromosomes. Mitosis is characteristic of eukaryotic cells. It ensures that the genetic information of the species and the individual is conserved. It also permits the multiplication of cells, which is necessary for the development, growth, and regeneration of the organism. The word "mitosis" comes from the Greek *mitos*, which means "thread," or "weave." ●

NUCLEUS

CHROMATIN

CYTOPLASM

Antioxidants

Antioxidants are various types of substances (vitamins, enzymes, minerals, etc.) that combat the pernicious effects of free radicals—molecules that are highly reactive and form as a result of oxidation (when an atom loses an electron), which is often caused by coming into contact with oxygen. A consequence of this oxidative action is the aging of the body. One action of antioxidants is the regulation of mitosis. Preventive geriatrics has focused on using antioxidants to prevent disease and to slow aging, in part because properly regulated mitosis is fundamental to these processes.

50,000

THE ESTIMATED NUMBER OF CELLS
REPLACED EVERY SECOND IN THE HUMAN
BODY THROUGH CELLULAR DIVISION

The Ever-Changing Skin

Mitosis, or cellular division, occurs intensely within the skin, a fundamental organ of the sense of touch. The dead cells on the surface are continuously being replaced by new cells, which are produced by mitosis in the lowest, or basal, layer. From there the cells move upward until they reach the epidermis, the outer layer of the skin. A person typically sheds 30,000 dead skin cells every minute.

SHEDDING SUPERFICIAL CELLS   LAYERS OF THE SKIN

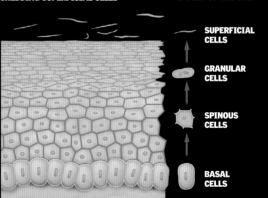

SUPERFICIAL
CELLS

GRANULAR
CELLS

SPINOUS
CELLS

BASAL
CELLS

1. **INTERPHASE**
An independent stage that precedes mitosis. The chromatin consists of DNA.

CHROMOSOME

2. **PROPHASE**
In prophase the chromatin condenses to form chromosomes. The karyotheca (nuclear envelope) begins to disappear. Chromosomes are formed by two chromatids that are joined together by a centromere.

CENTROMERE

3. **METAPHASE**
It is characterized by the appearance of the spindle. The centromere—the "center" of each chromosome—and the chromatids are joined together and align at the center of the spindle complex. The nuclear membrane disappears.

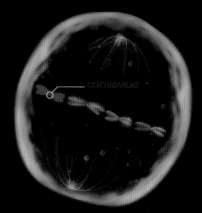

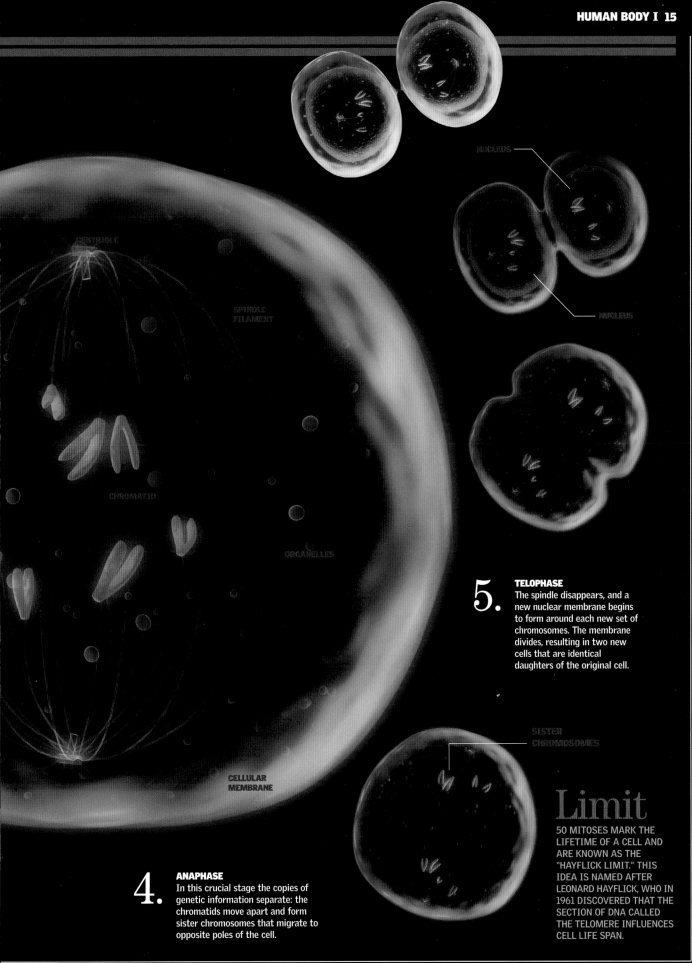

NUCLEUS

NUCLEUS

CENTRIOLE

SPINDLE
FILAMENT

CHROMATID

ORGANELLES

5. **TELOPHASE**
The spindle disappears, and a new nuclear membrane begins to form around each new set of chromosomes. The membrane divides, resulting in two new cells that are identical daughters of the original cell.

SISTER
CHROMOSOMES

CELLULAR
MEMBRANE

Limit

50 MITOSES MARK THE LIFETIME OF A CELL AND ARE KNOWN AS THE "HAYFLICK LIMIT." THIS IDEA IS NAMED AFTER LEONARD HAYFLICK, WHO IN 1961 DISCOVERED THAT THE SECTION OF DNA CALLED THE TELOMERE INFLUENCES CELL LIFE SPAN.

4. **ANAPHASE**
In this crucial stage the copies of genetic information separate: the chromatids move apart and form sister chromosomes that migrate to opposite poles of the cell.

Systems of the Body

The body has various systems with different functions. These functions range from reproducing a cell to developing a new human being, from circulating the blood to capturing oxygen from the air, and from processing food through grinding and chemical transformations to absorbing nutrients and discarding waste. These functions act in harmony, and their interaction is surprisingly efficient. ●

Circulatory System

This system carries blood to and from the heart and reaches the organs and cells in every part of the body. The supreme pump—the heart—drives the vital fluid—blood—through the arteries and collects it by means of the veins, with a continuous driving impulse that makes the heart the central engine of the body. **See page 36.**

Skeletal System

The skeleton, or skeletal system, is a solid structure consisting of bones that are supported by ligaments and cartilage. The main functions of the system are to give the body form and to support it, to cover and protect the internal organs, and to allow motion to occur. The skeleton also generates red blood cells (called erythrocytes). **See page 20.**

Nervous System

The central nervous system consists of the brain, which is the principal organ of the body, along with the spinal cord. The peripheral nervous system consists of the cranial and spinal nerves. Together they send external and internal sensations to the brain, where the sensations are processed and responded to whether the person is asleep or awake. **See page 82.**

Reproductive System

FEMALE

A woman's internal organs are the vagina, the uterus, the ovaries, and the fallopian tubes. The basic functions of these organs are the production of ova and the facilitation of fertilization of an ovum by a spermatozoon (a mature male sperm cell). When fertilization occurs, it sets a group of processes in motion that result in pregnancy. **See page 66.**

Lymphatic System

Its basic functions are twofold. One is to defend the body against foreign organisms, such as bacteria or viruses. The other is to transport interstitial fluid and substances from the digestive system into the bloodstream via the lymphatic drainage system. **See page 42.**

Respiratory System

Air from the external world enters the body through the upper airways. The central organs, the lungs, absorb oxygen and expel carbon dioxide. The lungs send oxygenated blood to all the cells via the circulatory system and in turn receive blood that requires purification. **See page 46.**

Endocrine System

The endocrine system is formed by glands that are distributed throughout the body. Its primary function is to produce approximately 50 hormones, the body's chemical messengers. The endocrine system secretes the hormones into the bloodstream so that they can reach the organs they are designed to influence, excite, or stimulate for such activities as growth and metabolism. **See page 62.**

MALE

The various male organs contribute one of the two cells needed to create a new human being. Two testicles (or gonads) and a penis are the principal organs of the system. The system is continuously active, producing millions of tiny cells called spermatozoa. **See page 64.**

Muscular System

Its function is to define the shape of the organism and protect it. The muscular system is essential for producing movement. It consists of muscles, organs made of fleshy tissue, and contractile cells. There are two types of muscles: striated and smooth. Striated muscles are attached to the bones and govern voluntary movement. Smooth muscles also obey the brain, but their movement is not under voluntary control. The myocardium, the muscle tissue of the heart, is unique and is in a class by itself. **See page 30.**

Digestive System

This system is a large tract that changes form and function as it goes from the mouth to the rectum and anus, passing through the pharynx, the esophagus, the stomach, and the small and large intestines. The liver and pancreas help process ingested food to extract its chemical components. Some of these components are welcome nutrients that are absorbed by the system, but others are useless substances that are discarded and eliminated. **See page 50.**

Urinary System

This system is a key system for homeostasis—that is, the equilibrium of the body's internal conditions. Its specific function is to regulate the amount of water and other substances in the body, discarding any that are toxic or that form an unnecessary surplus. The kidneys and the bladder are the urinary system's principal organs. The ureters transport the urine from the kidneys to the bladder, and the urethra carries the urine out of the body. **See page 58.**

Bones and Muscles

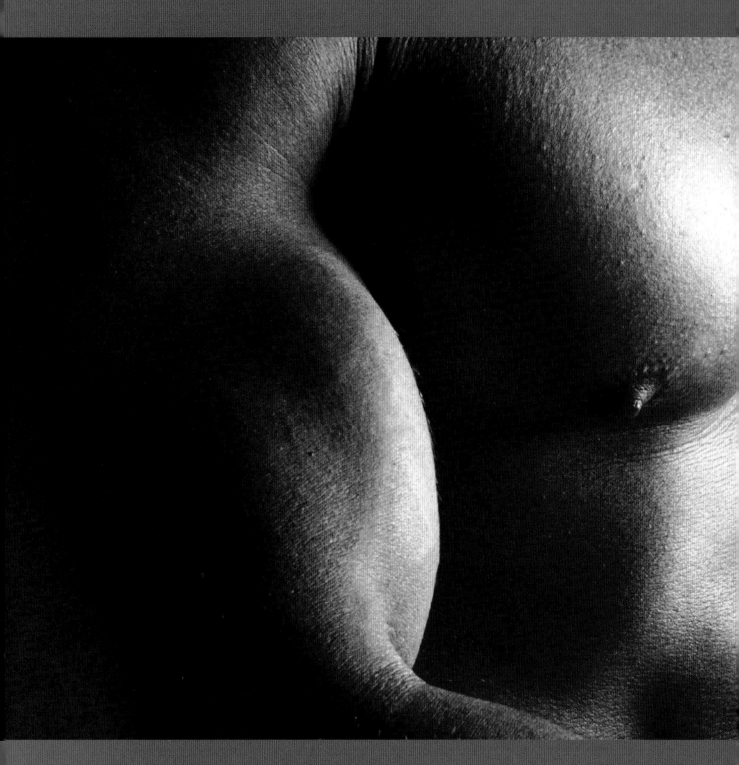

The musculoskeletal system consists of the skeletal system of bones, attached to each other by ligaments to form joints, and the skeletal muscles, which use tendons to attach muscles to bone. The skeleton gives resistance and stability to the body and serves as a support structure for the muscles to work and produce movement. The bones also

MUSCLES OF THE THORAX
They play an important role in
breathing by facilitating the
contraction and expansion of
the thoracic cavity.

SKELETON 20-21

BONE TISSUE 22-23

CRANIUM AND FACE 24-25

THE GREAT AXIS OF THE BODY 26-27

JOINTS 28-29

MUSCULAR SYSTEM 30-31

MUSCLE FIBER 32-33

serve as a shield to protect the internal
organs. In this chapter you will see in
detail—even down to the inside of a
muscle fiber—how each part works.
Did you know that bones are constantly
being regenerated and that, besides
supporting the body, they are charged
with producing red blood cells? In this
chapter you will find incredible images,
curiosities, and other information. ●

Skeleton

The skeleton, or the skeletal system, is a strong, resistant structure made up of bones and their supporting ligaments and cartilage. The skeleton gives the body form and structure, covers and protects the internal organs, and makes movement possible. The bones store minerals and produce blood cells in the bone marrow. ●

Well-Defined Form

The structure of the skeleton can be described as a vertical column of chained vertebrae with a pair of limbs at each end and topped off by the cranium. The upper limbs, or arms, are connected to the shoulder blades and clavicles in what is called the scapular belt, and the lower limbs, or legs, are connected at the hips, or pelvic belt. The joints reach such a level of perfection that modern engineering often uses them as a model in the study of levers when designing such objects as cranes or desk lamps. Although the bones that make up the skeleton are solid, they have a flexible structure and to a large degree consist of spongy tissue. Nevertheless, a small bone is capable of supporting up to 9 tons without breaking. A comparable weight would crush a block of concrete. For a long time anatomists thought that bones themselves were not alive and that their strength merely provided support for the other organs. Modern medicine recognizes that bones are actively living, furnished with nerves and supplied with blood.

Leonardo

In the Renaissance, the cradle of modernity, Leonardo da Vinci was one of the first to make precise drawings of human bones. Such drawings were needed for studying anatomy since there were no photographs or X-rays.

17 inches
(43 cm)

THE SIZE OF THE LARGEST BONE OF THE BODY, THE FEMUR

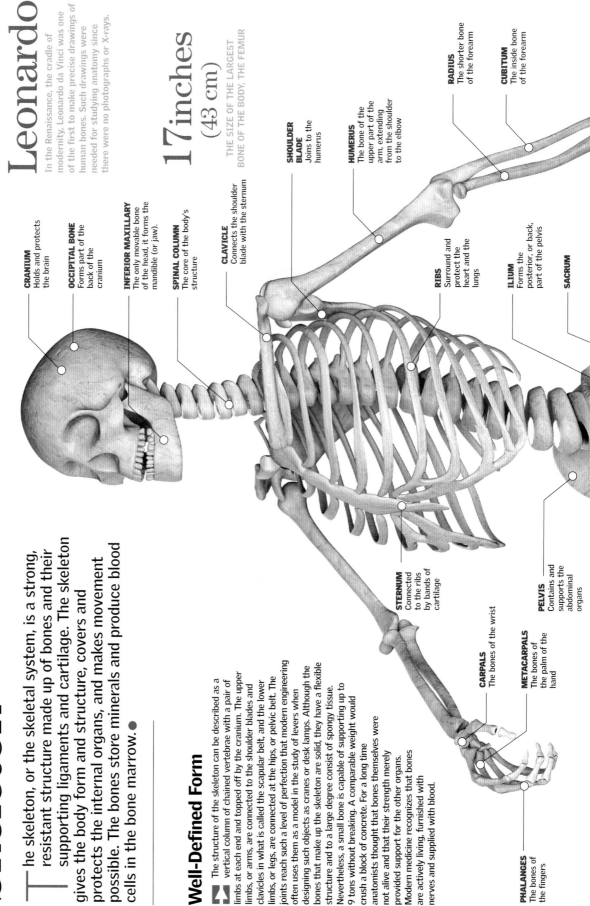

CRANIUM
Holds and protects the brain

OCCIPITAL BONE
Forms part of the back of the cranium

INFERIOR MAXILLARY
The only movable bone of the head, it forms the mandible (or jaw).

SPINAL COLUMN
The core of the body's structure

CLAVICLE
Connects the shoulder blade with the sternum

SHOULDER BLADE
Joins to the humerus

HUMERUS
The bone of the upper part of the arm, extending from the shoulder to the elbow

RADIUS
The shorter bone of the forearm

CUBITUM
The inside bone of the forearm

RIBS
Surround and protect the heart and the lungs

ILIUM
Forms the posterior, or back, part of the pelvis

SACRUM

STERNUM
Connected to the ribs by bands of cartilage

PELVIS
Contains and supports the abdominal organs

CARPALS
The bones of the wrist

METACARPALS
The bones of the palm of the hand

PHALANGES
The bones of the fingers

Types of Bones

Depending on their characteristics, such as size or shape, the bones of the human body are generally classified as follows:

SHORT BONES: have a spherical or conical shape. The heel bone is a short bone.

LONG BONES: have a central section that lies between two end points, or epiphyses. The femur is a long bone.

FLAT BONES: form thin bony plates. Most bones of the cranium are flat bones.

IRREGULAR BONES: take various shapes. The sphenoids ("wedgelike" bones) in the skull are irregular bones.

SESAMOID BONES: are small and round. The patella and the bones between tendons and in the joints of the hands and feet are sesamoid bones.

Axial Bones

The body has 80 of these bones, which belong to the part of the skeleton formed by the spinal column, the ribs, and the cranium.

208 bones

The total number of bones in the body is between 206 and 208, depending on the individual. The variation occurs with the supernumerary bones (bones of the skull) and the sesamoids (bones found in the joints of the hands and feet or embedded within tendons).

TIBIA
The bone that supports most of the weight of the lower part of the leg

TARSALS
Ankle bones

METATARSALS
Five small bones between the ankle and the toes

Appendicular Bones

THESE COMPRISE THE OTHER 126 BONES: THOSE OF THE ARMS, SHOULDERS, HIPS, AND LEGS. THESE BONES PERMIT A GREAT RANGE OF MOTION.

0.12 inches (3 mm)

THE LENGTH OF THE SHORTEST BONE OF THE BODY. IT IS THE STIRRUP, A BONE IN THE EAR.

— COCCYX (TAILBONE)

CALCANUM
Heel bone, the largest bone of the foot

KNEECAP
The knee bone, or patella, which is enveloped by tendons

FEMUR
The thigh bone, the largest bone in the body. It extends from the hip to the knee.

FIBULA
The thin outside bone of the lower part of the leg

PHALANGES
Bones of the toes

Sexual Differences

Bone structure is basically the same for both sexes. In women, though, the center opening of the pelvis is larger in order for an infant's head to pass through it during childbirth. The pelvic girdle is formed by two coxal, or hip, bones, which are joined in the rear with the sacral bone and are fused together in the front in the pubis. The pelvic girdle is involved in the joining of the hips, where it connects to the femur (thigh bone), serving the function of transmitting weight downward from the upper part of the body. The pelvic girdle and sacrum form the pelvis, which contains the organs of the digestive, reproductive, and urinary systems.

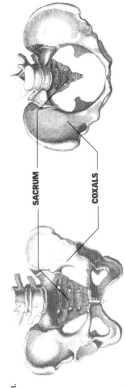

SACROILIAC
The joint that transmits the weight of the body from the spinal column to the pelvis

SACRUM

COXALS

Bony Tissue

The primary mission of the bones is to protect the organs of the body. Bones are solid and resilient, which allows them to endure blows and prevent damage to the internal organs. The hard exterior is balanced by the internal spongy part. Over a person's lifetime bones are continuously regenerated; this process continues even after a person reaches maturity. Besides supporting the body and enabling movement, the bones are charged with producing red globules: thousands of millions of new cells are produced daily in the bone marrow, in a never-ending process of replacing old cells. ●

Calcium and Marrow

All the hard parts that form the skeleton in vertebrates, such as the human being, are called bones. They may be hard, but they are nevertheless formed by a structure of living cells, nerves, and blood vessels, and they are capable of withstanding pressure of up to 1,000 pounds (450 kg). Because of their constitution and characteristics, they can mend themselves when fractured. A resistant exterior layer called the periosteum covers the outside of the compact bone. The endosteum, a thin layer of connective tissue lining the interior cavity of bone, contains the trabecular, or spongy mass, which is characterized by innumerable pores. The bone marrow, located in the center of the large bones, acts as a virtual red blood-cell factory and is also known as the medulla ossea. Minerals such as calcium go into making the bones. The fact that calcium is found in foods such as milk explains why healthy bones are usually associated with drinking a lot of milk. Calcium and phosphorous, among other chemical substances, give bones strength and rigidity. Proteins such as collagen provide flexibility and elasticity.

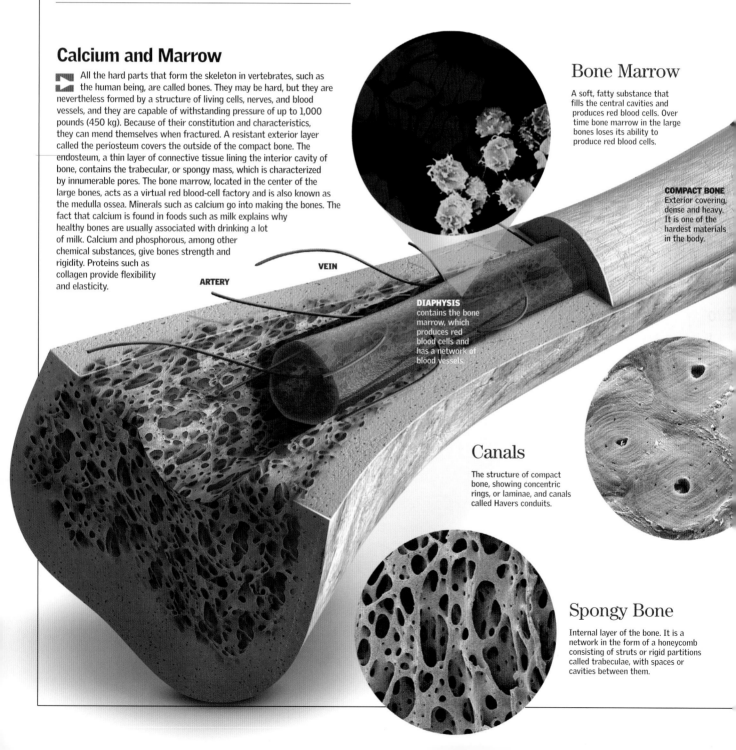

Bone Marrow

A soft, fatty substance that fills the central cavities and produces red blood cells. Over time bone marrow in the large bones loses its ability to produce red blood cells.

COMPACT BONE
Exterior covering, dense and heavy. It is one of the hardest materials in the body.

VEIN

ARTERY

DIAPHYSIS
contains the bone marrow, which produces red blood cells and has a network of blood vessels.

Canals

The structure of compact bone, showing concentric rings, or laminae, and canals called Havers conduits.

Spongy Bone

Internal layer of the bone. It is a network in the form of a honeycomb consisting of struts or rigid partitions called trabeculae, with spaces or cavities between them.

TWO TYPES OF BONE CELLS

The osseous tissue consists of two types of cells, osteoblasts and osteoclasts. Both are produced by the bone marrow, and their interaction and equilibrium ensure the integrity and continuous renewal of the bone. An osteoclast reabsorbs bone tissue, leaving empty spaces, and an osteoblast fills them. The function of the osteocytes, a variant of the osteoblasts, is to maintain the shape of the bone.

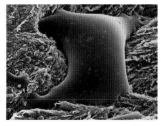

OSTEOBLAST produces osseous, or bone, tissue, which maintains the strength of the bone.

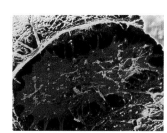

OSTEOCLAST breaks down the tissue so that it can be replaced with newer tissue.

BLOOD VESSELS carry blood to and from the bones to the rest of the body.

PERIOSTEUM A thin membrane that covers the exterior surface of the bone

WHY FRACTURES HEAL

Bone has great regenerative capacity. Bone tissue has an extraordinary ability to repair itself after a fracture through processes that include the relatively rapid generation of cells. Medicine can guide these processes to cure other lesions, deformities, etc.

A A fracture occurs, and the blood cells coagulate to seal the broken blood vessels.

C Within one to two weeks new spongy bone develops on a base of fibrous tissue. The spaces created by the fracture are filled, and, finally, the ends are fused.

B Over a few days a fibrous mesh forms, which closes the ends of the bone and replaces the coagulate.

D Within two to three months, new blood vessels have developed. Compact bone forms on the bony callous.

Evolution of Bone

Bone development is completed at about 18 or 20 years of age in a process that begins with an infant's bones, which are largely cartilage, and continues with the ongoing generation of bone in the person as an adult. Calcium is an indispensable element for the healthy development of bones through this process. Until the age of six months, an intake of 0.007 ounce (210 mg) of calcium per day is recommended.

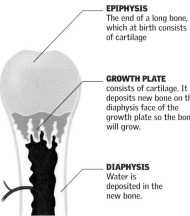

EPIPHYSIS The end of a long bone, which at birth consists of cartilage

GROWTH PLATE consists of cartilage. It deposits new bone on the diaphysis face of the growth plate so the bone will grow.

DIAPHYSIS Water is deposited in the new bone.

EPIPHYSIS Secondary ossification centers, to aid in long-term bone growth and to shape the bones

GROWTH PLATE Continues to act, depositing bone on the diaphysis face of the growth plate

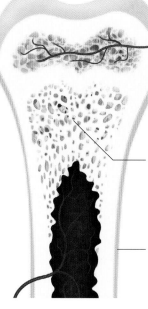

FUSION Epiphysis, growth plates, and diaphysis are transformed into continuous bone.

DIAPHYSIS Also called "bone shaft"

1 IN AN INFANT In a newborn infant the ends of the long bone (epiphyses) are made of cartilage. Between the bone shaft and an epiphysis, an area called a "growth plate" produces cartilage to lengthen the bone.

2 IN A CHILD In a child ossification continues to completion during epiphysis, generating long-term bone growth.

3 IN AN ADULT The process is complete when a person reaches about 18 years of age. The epiphysis, growth plates, and bone shaft fuse and become ossified into a continuous bone.

Cranium and Face

The cranium surrounds and protects the brain, cerebellum, and cerebral trunk (sometimes called the encephalus). In an adult the cranium consists of eight bones that form the skull and the base of the cranium. The face is the anterior part of the skull. It consists of 14 bones, all of which are fixed except the lower maxillary, which makes up the mandible. The total number of bones in the head as a whole exceeds the total of the face and cranium (22) because it includes the little bones of the middle ear. ●

Sutures and Fontanels

The cranium can be compared to a sphere, which consists of separate bones at birth and closes completely at maturity. The narrow separations between the bones, which appear as lines in the fetus for the first months of its life, are called sutures. Spaces called fontanels form where the sutures meet. Their separation has the functional purpose of allowing the brain to grow. Therefore, when brain growth is complete, the sphere closes tightly, because its function is to protect the brain.

Vibration

When a person speaks, the bones of the cranium vibrate. In Japan a technology was developed based on this vibration. In 2006 the firefighters of the Madrid municipality in Spain adopted this technology. A helmet, furnished with a cranial contact microphone, amplifies the vibrations produced in the bones of the cranium during speech and sends them to radio equipment.

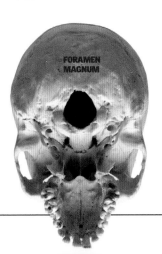

FORAMEN MAGNUM

Foramen Magnum

In Latin this term means "big hole." It is a circular opening, also called the occipital orifice, which is located at the base of the cranium. The foramen magnum allows for the passage of the spinal column, the medulla oblongata, the vertebral arteries, and the spinal nerve. The placement of the foramen magnum toward the bottom of the skull is associated with more highly evolved species.

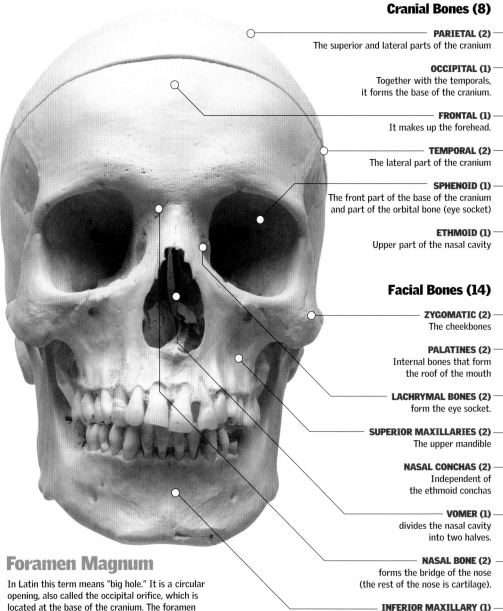

Cranial Bones (8)

PARIETAL (2)
The superior and lateral parts of the cranium

OCCIPITAL (1)
Together with the temporals, it forms the base of the cranium.

FRONTAL (1)
It makes up the forehead.

TEMPORAL (2)
The lateral part of the cranium

SPHENOID (1)
The front part of the base of the cranium and part of the orbital bone (eye socket)

ETHMOID (1)
Upper part of the nasal cavity

Facial Bones (14)

ZYGOMATIC (2)
The cheekbones

PALATINES (2)
Internal bones that form the roof of the mouth

LACHRYMAL BONES (2)
form the eye socket.

SUPERIOR MAXILLARIES (2)
The upper mandible

NASAL CONCHAS (2)
Independent of the ethmoid conchas

VOMER (1)
divides the nasal cavity into two halves.

NASAL BONE (2)
forms the bridge of the nose (the rest of the nose is cartilage).

INFERIOR MAXILLARY (1)
constitutes the mandible and is the only facial bone that can move freely.

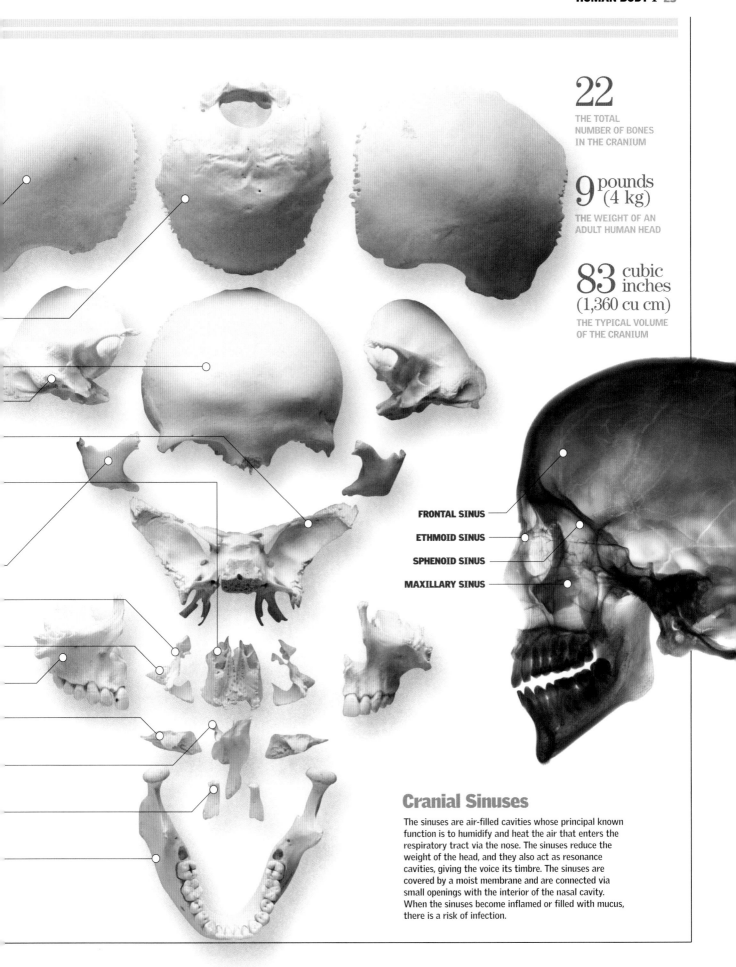

FRONTAL SINUS

ETHMOID SINUS

SPHENOID SINUS

MAXILLARY SINUS

Cranial Sinuses

The sinuses are air-filled cavities whose principal known
function is to humidify and heat the air that enters the
respiratory tract via the nose. The sinuses reduce the
weight of the head, and they also act as resonance
cavities, giving the voice its timbre. The sinuses are
covered by a moist membrane and are connected via
small openings with the interior of the nasal cavity.
When the sinuses become inflamed or filled with mucus,
there is a risk of infection.

The Great Axis of the Body

The vertebral, or spinal, column is the flexible axis that lends support to the body. It consists of a series of bones jointed together in a line, or chain, called the vertebrae. The spinal column forms a protective inner channel through which the spinal cord runs. The ribs perform a similar function, wrapping and shielding the vital internal organs, which include the heart and lungs. ●

Stability and Motion

The vertebrae have a centrum that allows them to support the body's weight, each vertebra upon the next, as well as the weight of the rest of the body. The vertebrae also have extensions that allow them to articulate with other vertebrae or act as supports for the ligaments and the muscles. This system gives the axis of the body both strength and flexibility. In addition, most of the nerves of the peripheral system (that is, those responsible for voluntary movement, for pain, and for the sense of touch) are connected to the spinal cord inside the spinal column. In the centrum the vertebrae are separated from each other by intervertebral disks that are made of cartilage and have a gelatinous interior. When an intervertebral disk is damaged, some of this material can escape and pinch a nerve. This condition, called a herniated disk, can be very painful.

The Ribs and the Rib Cage

The 12 pairs of ribs, which also extend from the spinal column, protect the heart, lungs, major arteries, and liver. These bones are flat and curved. The seven upper pairs are called "true ribs," and they are connected to the sternum (a flat bone consisting of fused segments) by cartilage. The next two or three pairs (called "false ribs") are connected indirectly. The remaining pairs ("floating ribs") are not attached to the sternum. The rib cage, formed by the ribs and its muscles, is flexible: it expands and contracts during breathing.

33 bones

OR VERTEBRAE, MAKE UP THE SPINAL COLUMN. DEPENDING ON THE INDIVIDUAL, SOMETIMES THERE ARE 34. THEY ARE CONNECTED BY DISKS OF CARTILAGE THAT ACT AS SHOCK ABSORBERS. THE SACRUM AND THE COCCYX ARE

LUNG

RIB CARTILAGE

STERNUM

HEART

SPLEEN

LIVER

STOMACH

ATLAS
This bone is the first of the seven cervical bones; it unites the spinal column with the head.

AXIS
The second cervical vertebra. Together with the atlas, it permits the movement of the head.

CERVICAL
These seven vertebrae (including the atlas and the axis) support the head and the neck.

THORACIC, OR DORSAL, VERTEBRAE
There are 12, and they are joined to the ribs.

The Three Curves
The three types of natural curvature in the spinal column include cervical lordosis (forward, or inward, bending in the cervical region of the spine), kyphosis (outward bending of the thoracic region of the spine), and lumbar lordosis (forward bending of the lower back). Shown here is the right side of the spinal column.

PARTS OF THE VERTEBRAE

1. SPINAL APOPHYSIS
2. TRANSVERSE APOPHYSIS (2)
3. ARTICULAR APOPHYSIS (4) (2 SUPERIOR AND 2 INFERIOR)
4. LAMINAE (2)
5. PEDICULAE (2)
6. FORAMEN MAGNUM
7. BODY

Downwards

All the vertebrae except the cervical axis and atlas have a cylindrical body, which gives them a particular characteristic: as they approach the pelvis they tend to be longer and stronger.

LUMBAR VERTEBRAE
There are five of them, and they bear the weight of the upper part of the body.

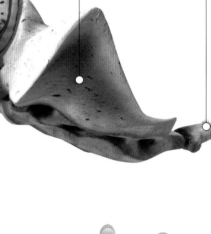

BLADE

SACRAL CANAL
Nerves pass through the sacral canal.

SACRUM
This bone is formed by five fused vertebrae.

COCCYX
This bone is composed of four fused vertebrae.

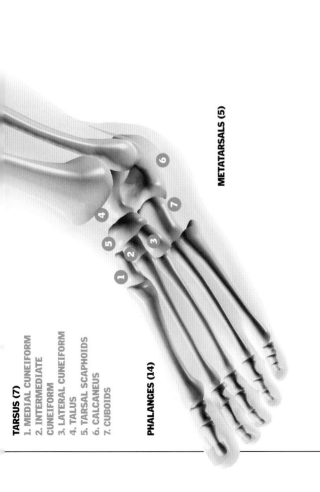

TARSUS (7)
1. MEDIAL CUNEIFORM
2. INTERMEDIATE CUNEIFORM
3. LATERAL CUNEIFORM
4. TALUS
5. TARSAL SCAPHOIDS
6. CALCANEUS
7. CUBOIDS

METATARSALS (5)

PHALANGES (14)

Bones of the Hands and Feet

Each hand (see the drawing below) has 27 bones, and each foot (see above) has 26. The hand has great mobility, and each of its fingers (five in all) has three phalanges (distal, medial, and proximal), except for the thumb, which has two. The complex of carpal bones makes up the wrist and is connected to the forearm. The metacarpal bone sustains the medial part. The feet function in a similar manner; the toes have first, second, and third phalanges, except for the big toe.

CARPALS (8)
1. LUNATE
2. PISIFORM
3. TRIQUETRUM
4. TRAPEZIUM
5. TRAPEZOID
6. CAPITATE
7. SCAPHOID
8. HAMATE

PHALANGES (14)

METACARPALS (5)

CARPALS (8)

Joints

They are the structures where two or more bones come together, either directly or by means of strong fibrous cords called ligaments. The skeleton has movement thanks to its joints. Most joints, like the knee, are synovial joints. They are characterized by mobility, versatility, and lubrication. The muscles that surround them contract to cause movement. When they work as a whole, the bones, muscles, and joints—together with the tendons, ligaments, and cartilage—constitute a grand system that governs the motor activity of the body and allows us to carry out our daily physical activities. ●

Hypermobility

The versatility of the joints refers to their characteristic range of motion. Just as there are mobile, semimobile, and fixed joints, there is also a group of joints that are hypermobile. Such joints are less common but are easily recognizable, especially in children and adults who have not lost the flexibility of their joints. The elbows, wrists, fingers, and knees can at an early age and in certain individuals have a greater-than-normal range of motion. For people with hypermobile joints this extra range of motion can be accomplished without difficulty or risk of dislocation.

Mobile

These are also called diarthroses; they are the joints with the greatest range of motion. The ends of the bones linked together are structured in various ways that facilitate their movement relative to each other, while ensuring the stability of the joint. Most joints in the body are of this type.

Semimobile

Also known as amphiarthroses. The surfaces of the bone that make contact have cartilaginous tissue. One example is the vertebral joints: they have little individual movement, but as a whole they have ample flexion, extension, and rotation.

Fixed

Also known as synarthroses. Most fixed joints are found in the cranium and have no need for motion because their primary function is to protect internal organs. They are connected by bone growth or fibrous cartilage and are extremely rigid and very tough.

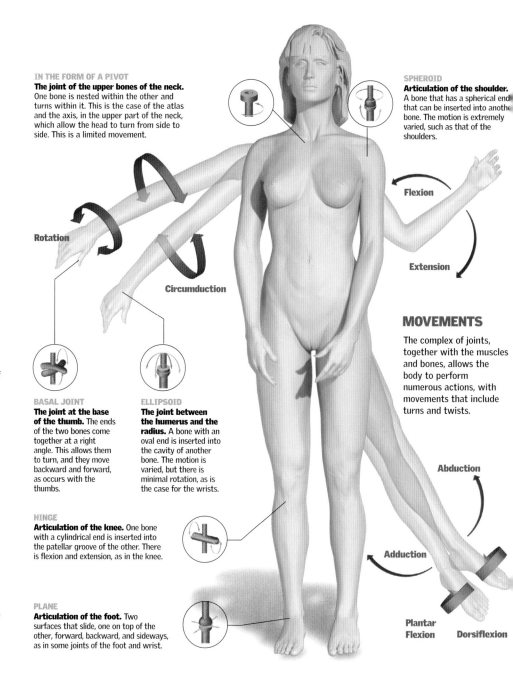

IN THE FORM OF A PIVOT
The joint of the upper bones of the neck. One bone is nested within the other and turns within it. This is the case of the atlas and the axis, in the upper part of the neck, which allow the head to turn from side to side. This is a limited movement.

Rotation

Circumduction

BASAL JOINT
The joint at the base of the thumb. The ends of the two bones come together at a right angle. This allows them to turn, and they move backward and forward, as occurs with the thumbs.

ELLIPSOID
The joint between the humerus and the radius. A bone with an oval end is inserted into the cavity of another bone. The motion is varied, but there is minimal rotation, as is the case for the wrists.

HINGE
Articulation of the knee. One bone with a cylindrical end is inserted into the patellar groove of the other. There is flexion and extension, as in the knee.

PLANE
Articulation of the foot. Two surfaces that slide, one on top of the other, forward, backward, and sideways, as in some joints of the foot and wrist.

SPHEROID
Articulation of the shoulder. A bone that has a spherical end that can be inserted into another bone. The motion is extremely varied, such as that of the shoulders.

Flexion

Extension

MOVEMENTS

The complex of joints, together with the muscles and bones, allows the body to perform numerous actions, with movements that include turns and twists.

Abduction

Adduction

Plantar Flexion

Dorsiflexion

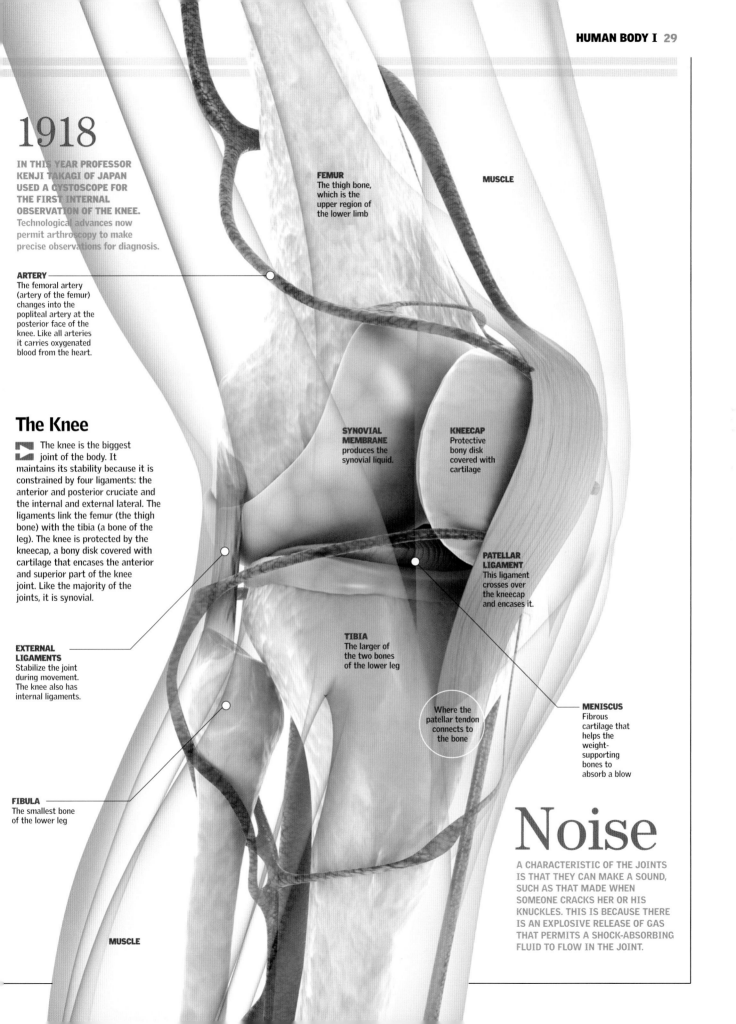

1918

IN THIS YEAR PROFESSOR KENJI TAKAGI OF JAPAN USED A CYSTOSCOPE FOR THE FIRST INTERNAL OBSERVATION OF THE KNEE. Technological advances now permit arthroscopy to make precise observations for diagnosis.

ARTERY
The femoral artery (artery of the femur) changes into the popliteal artery at the posterior face of the knee. Like all arteries it carries oxygenated blood from the heart.

The Knee

The knee is the biggest joint of the body. It maintains its stability because it is constrained by four ligaments: the anterior and posterior cruciate and the internal and external lateral. The ligaments link the femur (the thigh bone) with the tibia (a bone of the leg). The knee is protected by the kneecap, a bony disk covered with cartilage that encases the anterior and superior part of the knee joint. Like the majority of the joints, it is synovial.

EXTERNAL LIGAMENTS
Stabilize the joint during movement. The knee also has internal ligaments.

FIBULA
The smallest bone of the lower leg

MUSCLE

FEMUR
The thigh bone, which is the upper region of the lower limb

MUSCLE

SYNOVIAL MEMBRANE
produces the synovial liquid.

KNEECAP
Protective bony disk covered with cartilage

PATELLAR LIGAMENT
This ligament crosses over the kneecap and encases it.

TIBIA
The larger of the two bones of the lower leg

Where the patellar tendon connects to the bone

MENISCUS
Fibrous cartilage that helps the weight-supporting bones to absorb a blow

Noise

A CHARACTERISTIC OF THE JOINTS IS THAT THEY CAN MAKE A SOUND, SUCH AS THAT MADE WHEN SOMEONE CRACKS HER OR HIS KNUCKLES. THIS IS BECAUSE THERE IS AN EXPLOSIVE RELEASE OF GAS THAT PERMITS A SHOCK-ABSORBING FLUID TO FLOW IN THE JOINT.

Muscular System

T he muscles are organs formed by fleshy tissue consisting of contractile cells. They are divided into striated, smooth, and, in a unique case, cardiac (the myocardium is the muscular tissue of the heart). Muscles shape and protect the organism. The muscles of the skeleton are attached to the bones to permit voluntary movement, which is consciously directed by the brain. The smooth muscles are also directed by the brain, but their motion is not voluntary, as in the case of digestion. These muscles get most of their energy from alimentary carbohydrates, which can be stored in the liver and muscles in the form of glycogen and can later pass into the blood and be used as glucose. When a person makes a physical effort, there is an increased demand for both oxygen and glucose, as well as an increase in blood circulation. A lack of glucose leads to fatigue. ●

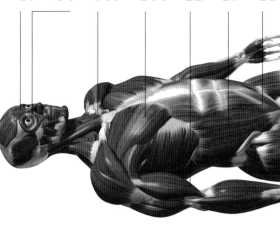

FRONTAL MUSCLE
wrinkles the forehead.

ORBICULAR MUSCLE
allows blinking.

STERNOCLEIDOMASTOID
allows the head to turn and move forward.

PECTORALIS MAJOR
stretches the arm forward. It turns it and brings it close to the body.

BRACHIAL BICEP
bends the arm at the elbow.

EXTERNAL OBLIQUE
turns the trunk and bends it to both sides.

RECTUS ABDOMINIS
bends the trunk forward.

OCCIPITAL
pulls the scalp backward.

DELTOID
A triangular muscle surrounding the shoulder. It lifts the arm to the side and causes it to swing when walking.

BRACHIAL TRICEP
stretches the arm at the elbow.

SPLENIUS
keeps the head erect.

TRAPEZIUM
turns the head and the shoulders forward. It stabilizes the shoulders.

When the Skeleton Moves

The great number of muscles of voluntary action available to the human body makes possible thousands of distinct movements. Actions from the simple blink of an eyelid to the twisting of a belt are accomplished by muscular action. The eye muscles involve the most activity because they carry out 100,000 movements per day. Some 30 muscles control all the movements of the face and define an infinite possible combination of facial expressions. It is calculated that to pronounce one word, the organs for speech and respiration move some 70 muscles. The stirrup muscle, which controls the stirrup of the ear, is one of the smallest in the body. It measures approximately 0.05 inch (1.2 mm). There are other muscles that are very large, including the latissimus dorsi of the shoulder. The foot has 40 muscles and more than 200 ligaments. Because the muscles are connected by a great number of nerves, a lesion or blow causes the brain to react,

producing pain. Approximately 40 percent of the total weight of the body consists of the muscular system. When the organism reduces the quantity of calories it normally ingests (for example, when a person goes on a diet), the first thing the body loses is water, which is reflected in a rapid weight loss. Then the metabolism adapts to the diet, and the body resorts to using up muscle tissue before drawing on the fats stored for burning calories. For this reason, when the diet begins this second phase, the consequences can be lack of vigor and loss of muscle tone, which is recovered when the diet returns to normal.

650 skeletal muscles

OR VOLUNTARY MUSCLES ARE IN THE TYPICAL HUMAN BODY.

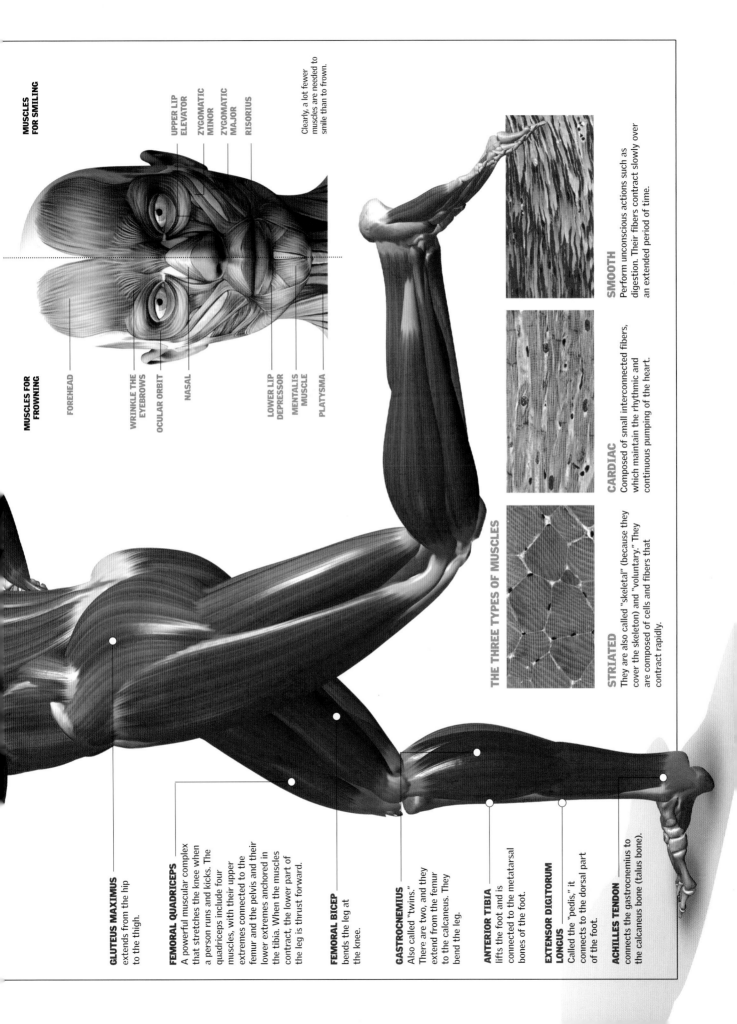

MUSCLES FOR SMILING

- UPPER LIP ELEVATOR
- ZYGOMATIC MINOR
- ZYGOMATIC MAJOR
- RISORIUS

Clearly, a lot fewer muscles are needed to smile than to frown.

MUSCLES FOR FROWNING

- FOREHEAD
- WRINKLE THE EYEBROWS
- OCULAR ORBIT
- NASAL
- LOWER LIP DEPRESSOR
- MENTALIS MUSCLE
- PLATYSMA

THE THREE TYPES OF MUSCLES

STRIATED
They are also called "skeletal" (because they cover the skeleton) and "voluntary." They are composed of cells and fibers that contract rapidly.

CARDIAC
Composed of small interconnected fibers, which maintain the rhythmic and continuous pumping of the heart.

SMOOTH
Perform unconscious actions such as digestion. Their fibers contract slowly over an extended period of time.

GLUTEUS MAXIMUS
extends from the hip to the thigh.

FEMORAL QUADRICEPS
A powerful muscular complex that stretches the knee when a person runs and kicks. The quadriceps include four muscles, with their upper extremes connected to the femur and the pelvis and their lower extremes anchored in the tibia. When the muscles contract, the lower part of the leg is thrust forward.

FEMORAL BICEP
bends the leg at the knee.

GASTROCNEMIUS
Also called "twins." There are two, and they extend from the femur to the calcaneus. They bend the leg.

ANTERIOR TIBIA
lifts the foot and is connected to the metatarsal bones of the foot.

EXTENSOR DIGITORUM LONGUS
Called the "pedis," it connects to the dorsal part of the foot.

ACHILLES TENDON
connects the gastrocnemius to the calcaneus bone (talus bone).

Muscular Fiber

A fiber is the long, thin cell that, when organized by the hundreds into groups called fascicles, constitutes the muscles. It is shaped like an elongated cylinder. The amount of fiber present varies according to the function accomplished by each muscle. Fibers are classified as white, which contract readily for actions that require force and power, and red, which perform slow contractions in movements of force and sustained traction. Each muscle fiber contains in its structure numerous filaments called myofibers. Myofibers, in turn, have two classes of protein filaments: myosin, also called thick filaments, and actin, or thin filaments. Both kinds of fibers are arranged in tiny matrices called sarcomeres. ●

Specialization

The quantity of muscle fiber varies according to the size and function of the muscle. Also, the same muscle can combine white fibers (rapid contracters) and red fibers (slow contracters). Even though their percentages differ from one person to the next, the composition of the muscles of the upper limbs tends to be the same as that of the lower in the same person. In other words, the relation between motor neurons and muscle fibers is inscribed in a person's genes. Depending on the type of neuron that stimulates them, the fibers are differentiated into slow fibers (when the neuron or motor neuron innervates between five and 180 fibers) and rapid fibers (when the neuron innervates between 200 and 800 fibers). The neurons and the fiber constitute what is called a motor unit.

Opposites

The muscles contract or relax according to the movement to be accomplished. To make the brain's directive take effect, the muscles involved carry out opposing actions.

CAPILLARIES
These bring blood to the muscle fibers.

FASCICLE
Each of the hundreds of fiber bundles that make up one muscle

MUSCLE FIBER

AXON
The extension of the nerve cell, whose end makes contact with the muscle and other cells

PERINEURIUM
The sheath of connective tissue that surrounds each fascicle

MUSCLE
Composed of hundreds of fiber bundles

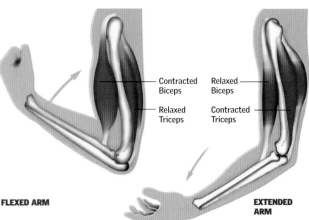

Contracted Biceps
Relaxed Triceps

Relaxed Biceps
Contracted Triceps

FLEXED ARM

EXTENDED ARM

12 inches (30 cm)
THE LENGTH A MUSCLE FIBER CAN REACH

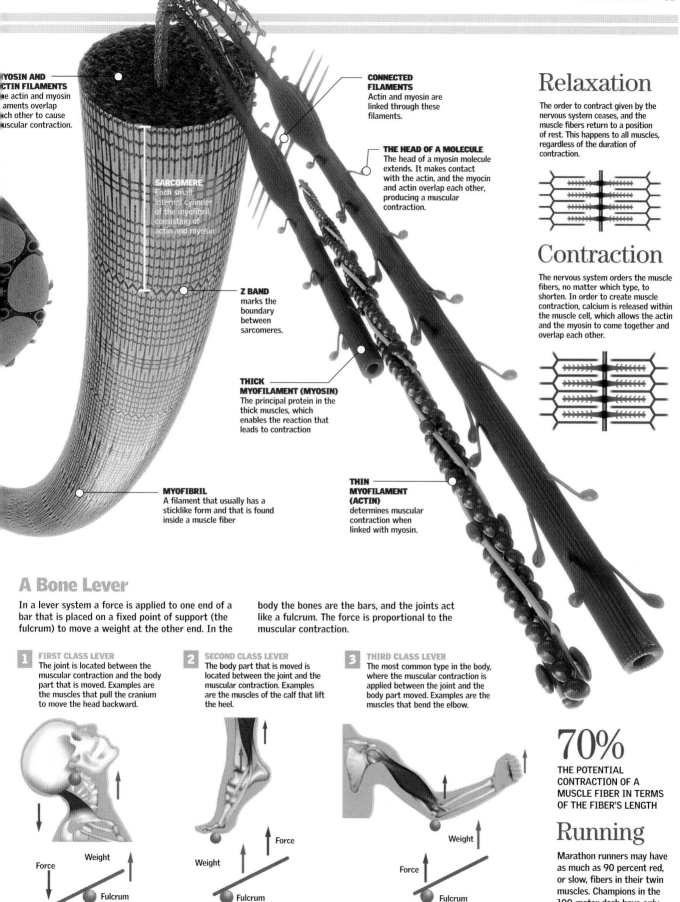

MYOSIN AND ACTIN FILAMENTS
The actin and myosin filaments overlap each other to cause muscular contraction.

CONNECTED FILAMENTS
Actin and myosin are linked through these filaments.

THE HEAD OF A MOLECULE
The head of a myosin molecule extends. It makes contact with the actin, and the myocin and actin overlap each other, producing a muscular contraction.

SARCOMERE
Each small internal cylinder of the myofibril, consisting of actin and myosin

Z BAND
marks the boundary between sarcomeres.

THICK MYOFILAMENT (MYOSIN)
The principal protein in the thick muscles, which enables the reaction that leads to contraction

THIN MYOFILAMENT (ACTIN)
determines muscular contraction when linked with myosin.

MYOFIBRIL
A filament that usually has a sticklike form and that is found inside a muscle fiber

Relaxation

The order to contract given by the nervous system ceases, and the muscle fibers return to a position of rest. This happens to all muscles, regardless of the duration of contraction.

Contraction

The nervous system orders the muscle fibers, no matter which type, to shorten. In order to create muscle contraction, calcium is released within the muscle cell, which allows the actin and the myosin to come together and overlap each other.

A Bone Lever

In a lever system a force is applied to one end of a bar that is placed on a fixed point of support (the fulcrum) to move a weight at the other end. In the body the bones are the bars, and the joints act like a fulcrum. The force is proportional to the muscular contraction.

1 FIRST CLASS LEVER
The joint is located between the muscular contraction and the body part that is moved. Examples are the muscles that pull the cranium to move the head backward.

2 SECOND CLASS LEVER
The body part that is moved is located between the joint and the muscular contraction. Examples are the muscles of the calf that lift the heel.

3 THIRD CLASS LEVER
The most common type in the body, where the muscular contraction is applied between the joint and the body part moved. Examples are the muscles that bend the elbow.

Force · Weight · Fulcrum

Weight · Force · Fulcrum

Force · Weight · Fulcrum

70%

THE POTENTIAL CONTRACTION OF A MUSCLE FIBER IN TERMS OF THE FIBER'S LENGTH

Running

Marathon runners may have as much as 90 percent red, or slow, fibers in their twin muscles. Champions in the 100-meter dash have only 20 to 25 percent.

Internal Systems and Organs

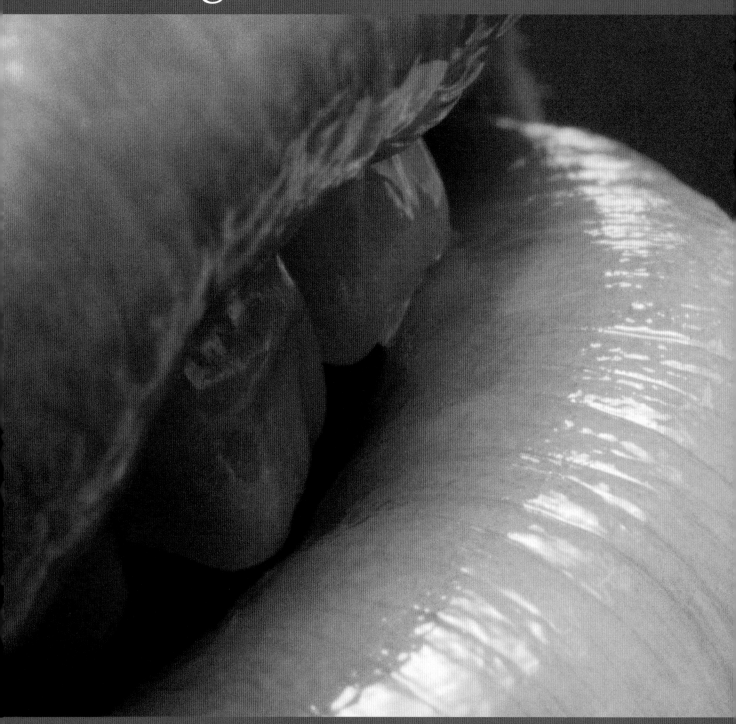

I t is difficult to explain that the sexual attraction between a man and woman—something that appears to be so natural and intimate—is a chemical phenomenon. What is certain is that when a couple feels they are in love, it is because hormones have gone into action. Without them, amorous thoughts and sexual fantasies would be drab and dull. We invite you to find out to

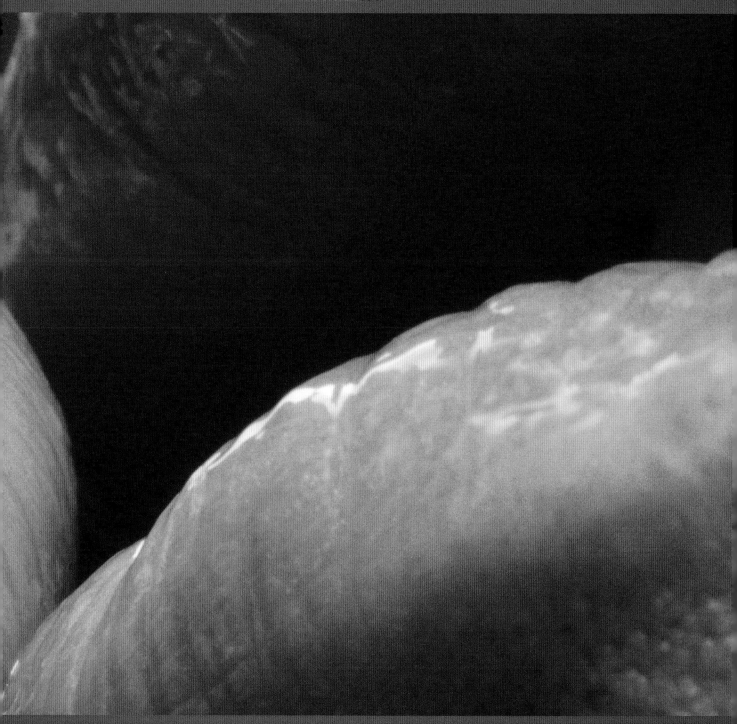

CIRCULATORY SYSTEM 36-37
ALL ABOUT THE HEART 38-39
COMPONENTS OF THE BLOOD 40-41
LYMPHATIC SYSTEM 42-43
GANGLIA 44-45
RESPIRATORY SYSTEM 46-47

LUNGS 48-49
DIGESTIVE SYSTEM 50-51
STOMACH 52-53
LIVER, PANCREAS, BILE 54-55
LARGE AND SMALL INTESTINE 56-57
URINARY SYSTEM 58-59

KIDNEYS 60-61
ENDOCRINE SYSTEM 62-63
MALE REPRODUCTIVE SYSTEM 64-65
FEMALE REPRODUCTIVE SYSTEM 66-67

what extent hormones determine many of our actions and also to investigate in detail, one by one, how the body's systems function. You will learn to understand how various organs of the body work as a team. Although each organ accomplishes specific tasks on its own, they all communicate with each other, and together they form a complete human being. ●

Circulatory System

I ts function is to carry blood to and from all the organs of the body. To drive the constant movement of the blood, the system uses the pumping of the heart, the organ that acts as the system's engine. The arteries bring oxygen-rich blood to all the cells, and the veins retrieve the blood so that it can be oxygenated once again and so that wastes can be removed. ●

A System That Goes Around

The center of the system is the heart, which, together with a network of vessels, forms the cardiovascular machinery. This vital engine beats more than 30 million times a year–approximately 2 billion times in a person's lifetime. With each beat it pumps about 5 cubic inches (82 ml) of blood. This means that an adult heart could fill a 2,000-gallon (8,000-l) tank in just one day. Beginning at the heart, the circulatory system completes two circuits: the main, or systemic, circulation via the aortic artery and the minor, or pulmonary, circulation. The main circulation brings oxygenated blood to the capillary system, where the veins are formed; the minor circulation brings oxygen-poor blood through the pulmonary artery to be enriched with oxygen and to have carbon dioxide removed from it, a process called hematosis. Other secondary circuits are the hepatic portal system and the hypophyseal portal system.

BLOOD DISTRIBUTION DURING CIRCULATION

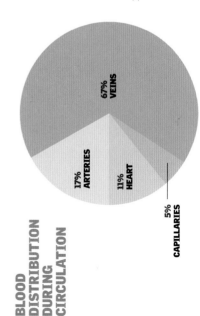

- 67% VEINS
- 17% ARTERIES
- 11% HEART
- 5% CAPILLARIES

1 inch (2.5 cm)

THE EXTERNAL DIAMETER OF THE AORTA (THE LARGEST ARTERY) AND THE VENA CAVA (THE LARGEST VEIN)

TEMPORAL ARTERY
runs along the side of the head.

TEMPORAL VEIN
runs along the side of the head.

JUGULAR VEINS
There are two on each side of the neck: the internal and the external.

LEFT CAROTID ARTERY
runs along the neck and supplies blood to the head.

AORTIC ARTERY (AORTA)
The body's principal artery

PULMONARY ARTERY
carries blood to the lungs.

HUMERAL ARTERY
(Axillary) The right one arises from the brachiocephalic trunk and the left from the aortic arch.

SUBCLAVIAN VEIN
connects the axillary with the superior vena cava.

RADIAL ARTERY
runs along the radial side of the forearm.

LEFT PRIMITIVE ILIAC ARTERY
provides blood to the pelvis and the legs.

LEFT PRIMITIVE

HEART
The great engine

SUPERIOR VENA CAVA
brings the blood from the upper part of the body for purification. The superior vena cava and the inferior vena cava together form the largest vein.

TRUNCUS OF THE PORTAL VEIN
It terminates in the sinusoids of the liver.

RENAL VEIN
Blood exits the kidneys through this vein.

INFERIOR VENA CAVA
takes blood arriving from the area below the diaphragm and brings it up to the heart.

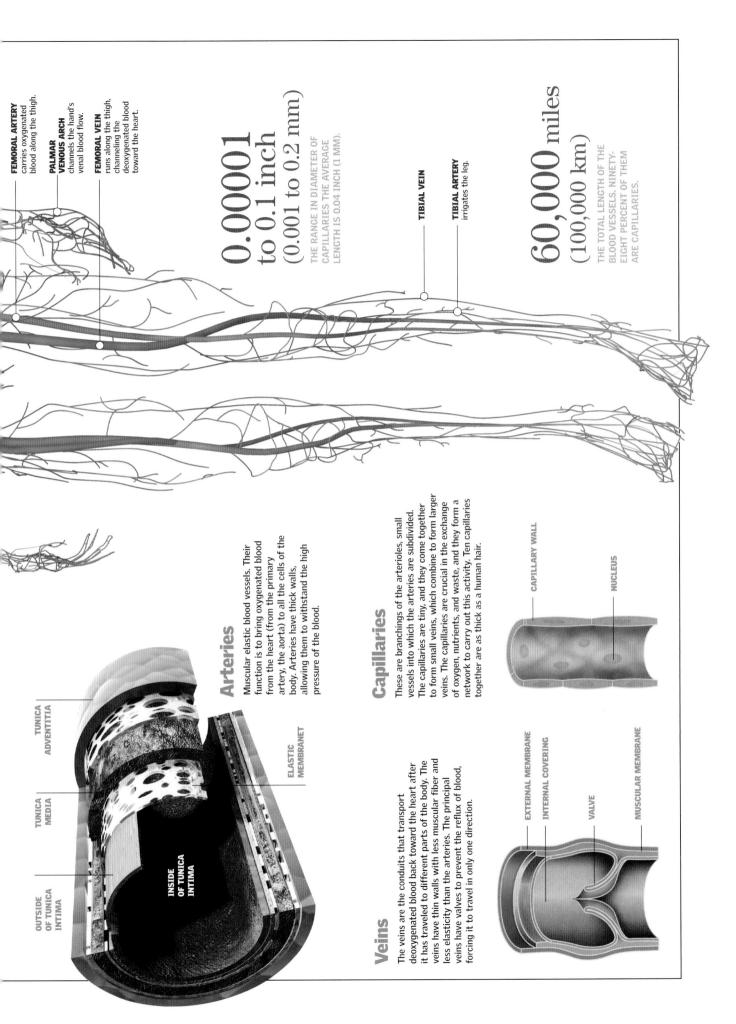

FEMORAL ARTERY
carries oxygenated
blood along the thigh.

**PALMAR
VENOUS ARCH**
channels the hand's
venal blood flow.

FEMORAL VEIN
runs along the thigh,
channeling the
deoxygenated blood
toward the heart.

0.00001 to 0.1 inch
(0.001 to 0.2 mm)

THE RANGE IN DIAMETER OF
CAPILLARIES THE AVERAGE
LENGTH IS 0.04 INCH (1 MM).

TIBIAL VEIN

TIBIAL ARTERY
irrigates the leg.

60,000 miles
(100,000 km)

THE TOTAL LENGTH OF THE
BLOOD VESSELS. NINETY-
EIGHT PERCENT OF THEM
ARE CAPILLARIES.

Arteries

Muscular elastic blood vessels. Their
function is to bring oxygenated blood
from the heart (from the primary
artery, the aorta) to all the cells of the
body. Arteries have thick walls,
allowing them to withstand the high
pressure of the blood.

Capillaries

These are branchings of the arterioles, small
vessels into which the arteries are subdivided.
The capillaries are tiny, and they come together
to form small veins, which combine to form larger
veins. The capillaries are crucial in the exchange
of oxygen, nutrients, and waste, and they form a
network to carry out this activity. Ten capillaries
together are as thick as a human hair.

CAPILLARY WALL

NUCLEUS

Veins

The veins are the conduits that transport
deoxygenated blood back toward the heart after
it has traveled to different parts of the body. The
veins have thin walls with less muscular fiber and
less elasticity than the arteries. The principal
veins have valves to prevent the reflux of blood,
forcing it to travel in only one direction.

**TUNICA
ADVENTITIA**

**ELASTIC
MEMBRANET**

**TUNICA
MEDIA**

**OUTSIDE
OF TUNICA
INTIMA**

**INSIDE
OF TUNICA
INTIMA**

EXTERNAL MEMBRANE

INTERNAL COVERING

VALVE

MUSCULAR MEMBRANE

All About the Heart

The heart is the engine of the circulatory apparatus: it supplies 10 pints (4.7 l) of blood per minute. Its rhythmic pumping ensures that blood arrives in every part of the body. The heart beats between 60 and 100 times per minute in a person at rest and up to 200 times per minute during activity. The heart is a hollow organ, the size of a fist; it is enclosed in the thoracic cavity in the center of the chest above the diaphragm. The name of the stomach's entrance, or cardias, comes from the Greek word for heart, *kardia*. Histologically, one can distinguish three layers of tissue in the heart, starting from the inside out: the endocardium, the myocardium, and the pericardium. ●

The Return Flow of Blood

These cells are phantom cells, because all they contain is a large amount of hemoglobin, a protein that has a great affinity for combining with oxygen. The red blood cells, which circulate in the blood, bring oxygen to the cells that need it, and they also remove a small part of the carbon dioxide that the cells are discarding as waste. Because they cannot reproduce themselves, they must be replaced by new red blood cells that are produced by the bone marrow.

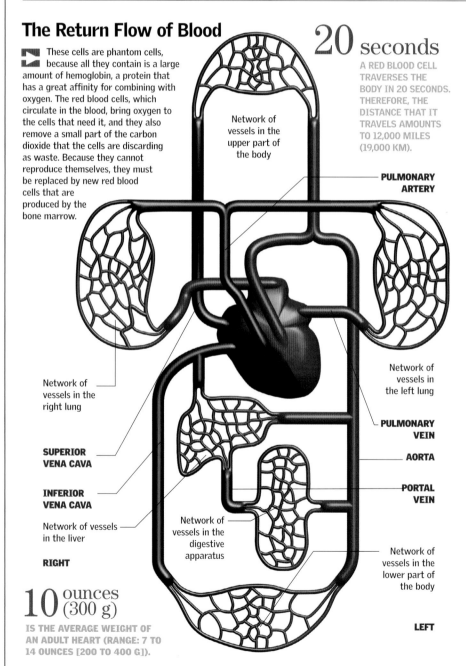

Network of vessels in the upper part of the body

20 seconds

A RED BLOOD CELL TRAVERSES THE BODY IN 20 SECONDS. THEREFORE, THE DISTANCE THAT IT TRAVELS AMOUNTS TO 12,000 MILES (19,000 KM).

PULMONARY ARTERY

Network of vessels in the right lung

Network of vessels in the left lung

PULMONARY VEIN

AORTA

PORTAL VEIN

SUPERIOR VENA CAVA

INFERIOR VENA CAVA

Network of vessels in the liver

Network of vessels in the digestive apparatus

Network of vessels in the lower part of the body

RIGHT

LEFT

10 ounces (300 g)

IS THE AVERAGE WEIGHT OF AN ADULT HEART (RANGE: 7 TO 14 OUNCES [200 TO 400 G]).

THE SEQUENCE OF THE HEARTBEAT

1 DIASTOLIC
The atria and the ventricles are relaxed. The blood, supercharged with carbon dioxide, flows from all the corners of the body and enters the right atrium, while the blood that was oxygenated through the work of the lungs returns to the left part of the heart.

2 ATRIAL SYSTOLE
The atria contract to push the blood down toward the ventricles. The right ventricle receives the blood that will have to be sent to the lungs to be oxygenated. The left ventricle receives blood coming from the lungs, which is already oxygenated and must be pumped toward the aorta.

3 VENTRICULAR SYSTOLE
The ventricles contract after a brief pause. The systole, or contraction, of the right ventricle sends impure blood to the lungs. The contraction of the left ventricle pumps the already oxygenated blood toward the aorta; it is ready for distribution throughout the body.

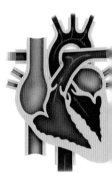

70

IS THE APPROXIMATE NUMBER OF TIMES THAT THE HEART BEATS PER MINUTE. IT PUMPS 2,000 GALLONS (8,000 L) OF BLOOD PER DAY.

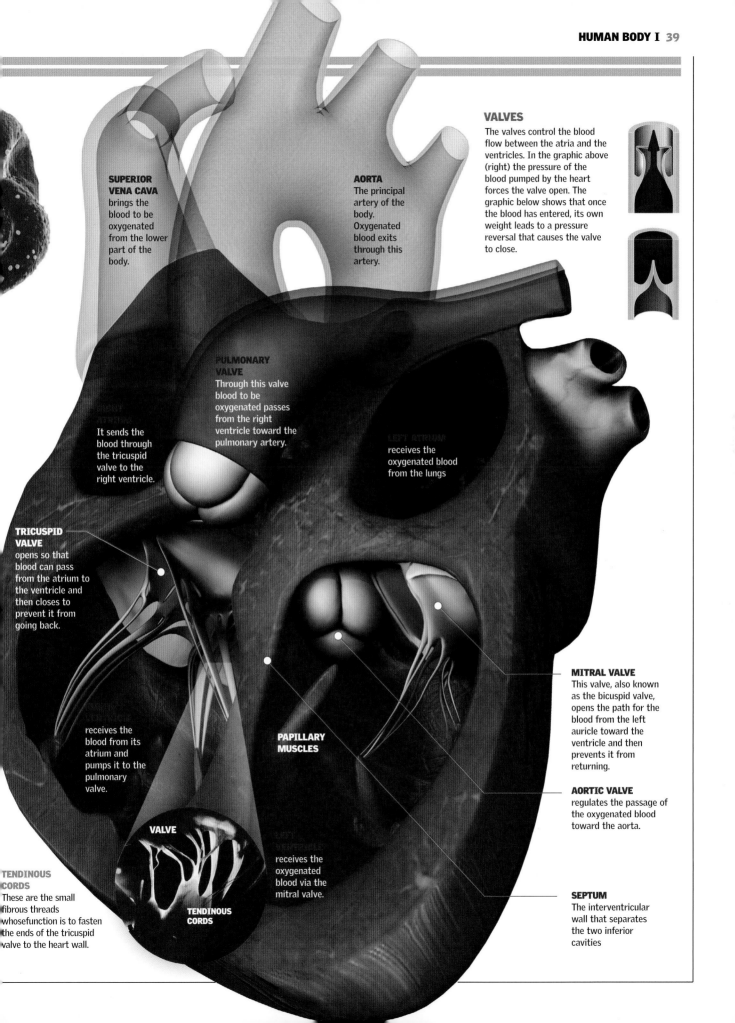

SUPERIOR VENA CAVA
brings the blood to be oxygenated from the lower part of the body.

AORTA
The principal artery of the body. Oxygenated blood exits through this artery.

VALVES
The valves control the blood flow between the atria and the ventricles. In the graphic above (right) the pressure of the blood pumped by the heart forces the valve open. The graphic below shows that once the blood has entered, its own weight leads to a pressure reversal that causes the valve to close.

PULMONARY VALVE
Through this valve blood to be oxygenated passes from the right ventricle toward the pulmonary artery.

RIGHT ATRIUM
It sends the blood through the tricuspid valve to the right ventricle.

LEFT ATRIUM
receives the oxygenated blood from the lungs

TRICUSPID VALVE
opens so that blood can pass from the atrium to the ventricle and then closes to prevent it from going back.

MITRAL VALVE
This valve, also known as the bicuspid valve, opens the path for the blood from the left auricle toward the ventricle and then prevents it from returning.

receives the blood from its atrium and pumps it to the pulmonary valve.

PAPILLARY MUSCLES

AORTIC VALVE
regulates the passage of the oxygenated blood toward the aorta.

VALVE

TENDINOUS CORDS

LEFT VENTRICLE
receives the oxygenated blood via the mitral valve.

TENDINOUS CORDS
These are the small fibrous threads whosefunction is to fasten the ends of the tricuspid valve to the heart wall.

SEPTUM
The interventricular wall that separates the two inferior cavities

Components of the Blood

The blood is a liquid tissue composed of water, dissolved substances, and blood cells. The blood circulates inside the blood vessels thanks to the impulse it receives from the contraction of the heart. A principal function of the blood is to distribute nutrients to all the cells of the body. For example, the red blood cells (erythrocytes) carry oxygen, which associates with the hemoglobin, a substance in the cell responsible for the blood's red color. The blood also contains white blood cells and platelets that protect the body in various ways. ●

Red Blood Cells

These cells are phantom cells, because all they contain is a large amount of hemoglobin, a protein that has a great affinity for combining with oxygen. The red blood cells, which circulate in the blood, bring oxygen to the cells that need it, and they also remove a small part of the carbon dioxide that the cells are discarding as waste. Because they cannot reproduce themselves, they must be replaced by new red blood cells that are produced by the bone marrow.

FLEXIBILITY
Red blood cells are flexible and take on a bell shape in order to pass through the thinnest blood vessels.

BICONCAVE FORM   BELL-SHAPED

5 quarts (4.7 l)
THE APPROXIMATE VOLUME OF BLOOD PRESENT IN A HUMAN ADULT

0.0003 INCH (0.008 MM)

The Blood Groups

Each person belongs to a blood group. Within the ABO system the groups are A, B, AB, and O. Each group is also identified with an antigen, or Rh factor, that is present in the red blood cells of 85 percent of the population. It is of vital importance to know what blood group a person belongs to so as to give only the right type during a blood transfusion. The immune system, via antibodies and antigens, will accept the body's own blood type but will reject the wrong type.

GROUP A
An individual with red blood cells with antigen A in its membranes belongs to blood group A, and that person's plasma has antibodies against type B. These antibodies recognize red blood cells with antigen B in their membranes as foreign.

ANTIGEN A

ANTI-B ANTIBODY

ANTIGEN B

GROUP B
Members of this group have antigen B in the membrane of their red blood cells and anti-A antibodies in their blood plasma.

ANTI-A ANTIBODY

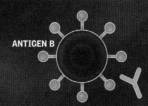

GROUP AB
Members of this group have antigen A and B in the membrane of their red blood cells and no antibodies in their blood plasma.

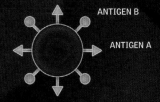
ANTIGEN B

ANTIGEN A

GROUP O
Members of this group have no antigens in the membranes of their erythrocytes and anti-A and anti-B antibodies in their blood plasma

ANTI-A ANTIBODY

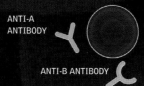

ANTI-B ANTIBODY

COMPATIBILITY
Donors of group O can give blood to any group, but group AB donors can give only to others with AB blood. The possibility of blood donation depends on the antibodies of the recipient.

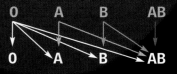
O   A   B   AB

O   A   B   AB

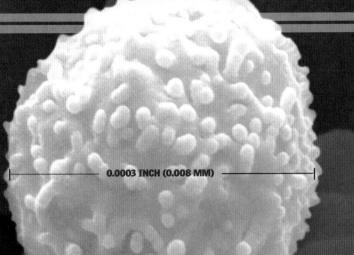

0.0003 INCH (0.008 MM)

White Blood Cells, or Leukocytes

This is what a leukocyte, or white blood cell, looks like swimming in blood plasma. They are called white because that is their color when viewed under a microscope.

7%

IS THE PORTION OF BODY WEIGHT REPRESENTED BY THE BLOOD.

COMPOSITION

GRANULOCYTES	Neutrophils
	Eosinophils
	Basophils
AGRANULOCYTES	Lymphocytes
	Monocytes

Blood Components

The blood is a tissue, and as such it is characterized by the same type of cells and intercellular substance as tissue. It is distinguished from the rest of the tissues in the human body by an abundance of intercellular material, which consists primarily of water. The intercellular material, called plasma, is yellow, and it contains abundant nutrients and other substances, such as hormones and antibodies, that take part in various physiological processes.

COMPONENTS OF THE BLOOD PER 0.00006 cubic inch (1 cu ml)

Red Blood Cells	4 to 6 million
White Blood Cells	4,500 to 11,000
Platelets	150,000 to 400,000
Normal pH	7.40

DAILY PRODUCTION IN MILLIONS

Red Blood Cells	200,000
White Blood Cells	10,000
Platelets	400,000

0.0003 INCH (0.008 MM)

③

Platelets

are cell fragments that have separated from the megakaryocytes, cells located in the bone marrow. They have a role in blood coagulation. Next to the red blood cells, the platelets are the most abundant component of the blood.

④

Plasma

Red and white blood cells and platelets (which contribute to coagulation) make up 45 percent of the blood. The remaining 55 percent is plasma, a fluid that is 90 percent water and the rest various nutrients.

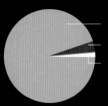

90% Water

8% Protein

2% other
(salts, nutrients, glucose, amino acid fats, and waste)

98.6° F (37° C)

THE BLOOD MAINTAINS THE BODY AT THIS AVERAGE TEMPERATURE.

Lymphatic System

It accomplishes two basic functions: defense against foreign organisms (such as bacteria) and aid with transport of liquid and matter via the circulation of the lymph from the interstices of the tissue and from the digestive apparatus to the blood. About 3 to 4 quarts (2.8-3.7 l) of the liquid circulating in the system do not return. This liquid is known as lymph, and it is reabsorbed into the plasma only through the lymphatic vessels. The lymph contains cells called lymphocytes and macrophages, which are part of the immune system. ●

Lymphatic Network

This network contains vessels that extend throughout the body and that filter the liquid that comes from the area surrounding the cells. The lymph circulates in only one direction and returns to the blood through the walls of small blood vessels. There are valves that prevent the lymph from flowing in the opposite direction. The lymph nodes filter harmful microorganisms from the lymph, which returns via blood vessels to maintain the equilibrium of the body's fluids. Together with the white blood cells, the lymph nodes are in charge of maintaining the immune system.

Lymphatic Tissue

One part of the liquid that exits from blood flow and distributes itself in the body returns only through the action of the lymphatic tissue, which reabsorbs it via the lymphatic capillaries and returns it to the blood via the lymphatic vessels.

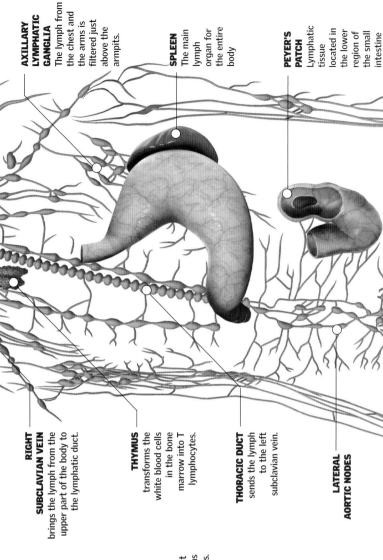

TONSILS
Similar to the ganglia, their tissue detects invading organisms.

LEFT SUBCLAVIAN VEIN
Has the same function as the right subclavian vein. The name derives from its location beneath the clavicle.

AXILLARY LYMPHATIC GANGLIA
The lymph from the chest and the arms is filtered just above the armpits.

SPLEEN
The main lymph organ for the entire body

PEYER'S PATCH
Lymphatic tissue located in the lower region of the small intestine

RIGHT SUBCLAVIAN VEIN
brings the lymph from the upper part of the body to the lymphatic duct.

THYMUS
transforms the white blood cells in the bone marrow into T lymphocytes.

THORACIC DUCT
sends the lymph to the left subclavian vein.

LATERAL AORTIC NODES

ARTERIOLE

BLOOD CAPILLARY

LYMPHATIC CELL

LYMPHATIC CAPILLARY

VENULE

DIRECTION OF BLOOD FLOW

BONE MARROW

The bone marrow generates white blood cells, or lymphocytes, within the bones.

6 gallons (24 l)

THE AMOUNT OF LIQUID THAT LEAVES THE BLOOD AND PASSES THROUGH THE SYSTEM DAILY, MOVING THROUGH THE TISSUES AND RETURNING TO THE BLOODSTREAM

SPLEEN

The largest lymphatic organ, it performs specific tasks, such as filtering the blood, producing white blood cells, and eliminating old blood cells. It also stores blood. The spleen can weigh between 3 and 9 ounces (100 and 250 g). It is about 5 inches (12 cm) long and 3 inches (7 cm) wide.

THYMUS

A gland consisting of two lobes, located in the upper section of the sternum. It develops during puberty and then begins to decline, transforming itself into a mass of connective tissue. The thymus transforms blood cells produced in the bone marrow into specialized T lymphocytes.

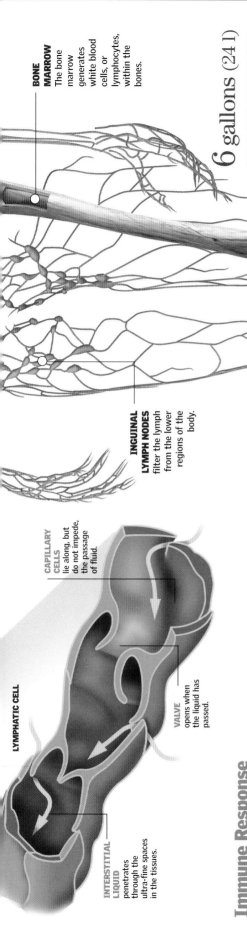

CAPILLARY CELLS lie along, but do not impede, the passage of fluid.

LYMPHATIC CELL

VALVE opens when the liquid has passed.

INTERSTITIAL LIQUID penetrates through the ultra-fine spaces in the tissues.

INGUINAL LYMPH NODES filter the lymph from the lower regions of the body.

POPLITEAL LYMPH NODES are located behind the knees, and they filter the lymph from the lower extremities.

LYMPHATIC VESSELS receive the lymph from the lymphatic capillaries.

BONE MARROW

Together with the thymus and the spleen, bone marrow constitutes the lymphatic system tissues, whose function is to mature the lymphocytes.

Immune Response

1. The lymphatic system generates lymphocytes (also found in the blood and in other tissue) and macrophages. Together they constitute the immune system. Here invading bacteria are devoured by a macrophage, and the B lymphocytes take information from the surface of the bacteria that they need to "recognize" other similar bacteria.

2. The B lymphocytes are activated and upon recognizing a pathogen divide themselves into plasmatic cells and memory cells. The plasmatic cells secrete thousands of antibody molecules per second, which are carried by the blood to the site of the infection. The memory cells retain the antigen information, and, when faced with a new invasion, will once again divide rapidly in order to deal with it.

3. The antibodies, also called "immunoglobin," are protein molecules in the form of a "Y," with arms unique to each specific type of antibody. It is this feature that attaches them to a specific antigen. Their function is to "mark" invaders, which can then be destroyed by the macrophages.

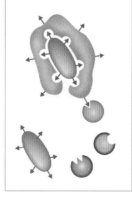
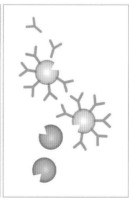
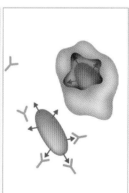

Lymph Node

A lso called a lymph gland, this node has a round shape and is about 0.4 inch (1 cm) in diameter. Lymph nodes are distributed throughout the body—in the neck, armpits, groin, and popliteal bone (behind the knees), as well as in the thorax and abdomen. The lymphatic vessels are the ducts for the lymph and the pathways for communication among the lymph nodes. The battle of the immune system against invading germs takes place within the nodes, which then enlarge because of inflammation. ●

A Defensive Filter

The glands are covered with a sheath of connective tissue, which in turn forms an interior network that consists of clusters filled with lymphocytes. Their immunological functions are to filter the fluid that arriv via both the sanguine and lymphatic afferent veins, which then goes toward heart to be returned to circulation via th efferent vessels and to produce immune cells for attacking and removing bacteria and carcinogenic cells.

Natural Defenses

Besides the immune system, composed in part by the lymphatic system, the body has another group of resources called natural defenses, which people possess from birth. The body's first defensive barrier is the skin. If pathogenic agents succeed in passing through its filters, however, both the blood and the lymph possess specialized antimicrobial cells and chemical substances.

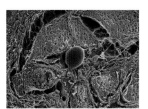

LACHRYMAL GLAND
Secretes tears that protect the eyes. Tears, like saliva and perspiration, kill bacteria.

100 square inches (600 sq cm)

THE AREA OF THE SKIN COVERED BY SWEAT GLANDS, A PART OF THE NATURAL DEFENSES THAT COMPLEMENT THE WORK OF THE GANGLIA IN THE IMMUNE SYSTEM

GERMINAL CENTER
The area that contains B lymphocytes. There are two types: B cells, which produce antibodies, and T cells.

SEBACEOUS GLAND
Located on the surface of the skin, this gland secretes a fatty substance called sebo.

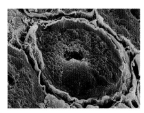

SALIVARY GLAND
produces saliva, which contains bactericidal lysozymes.

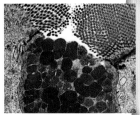

INTESTINAL MUCOSA
The goblet cells in this membrane produce a defensive mucus.

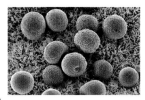

MUCOUS SECRETIONS
These secretions, called mucus, form in the upper and lower respiratory tracts, where they capture bacteria and carry them to the throat to be spit out.

MACROPHAGES
Together with the lymphocytes, they the basis of the in system. They devo invading bodies th detected.

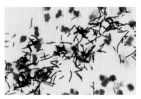

VAGINAL BACTERIA
Under normal conditions, these are inoffensive, and they occupy areas that could be invaded by pathogenic bacteria.

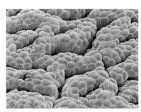

SWEAT GLAND
secretes sweat, which helps to control body temperature, to eliminate toxins, and to protect the skin immunologically.

AFFERENT LYMPHATIC VESSEL
The afferent vessels carry the lymphatic liquid from the blood to the ganglia, or lymphatic nodes.

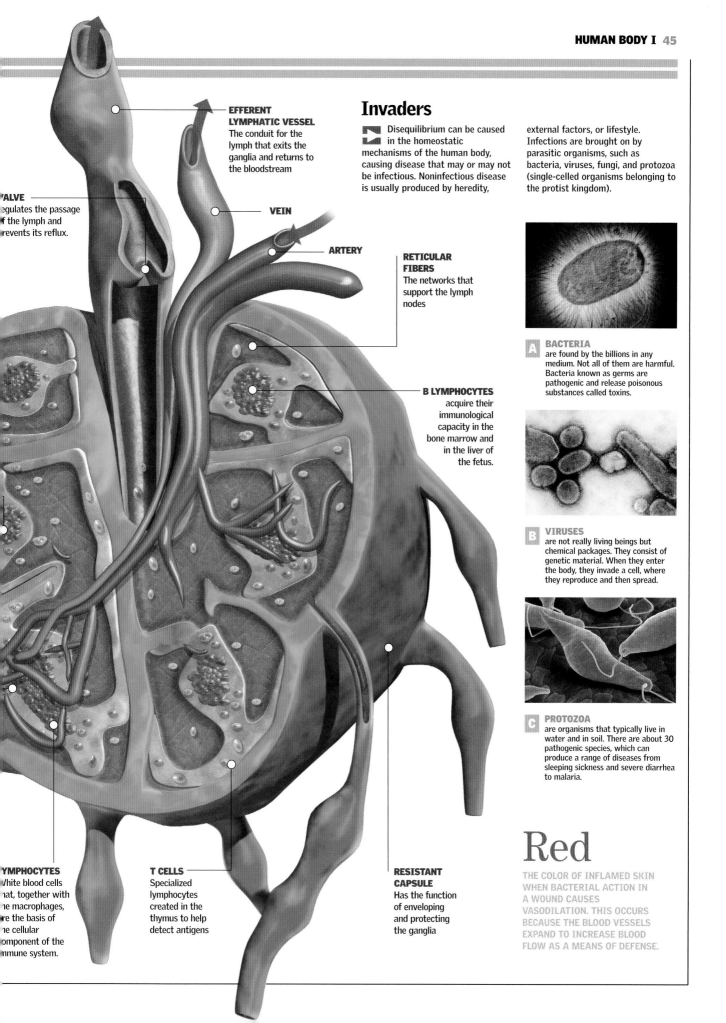

EFFERENT LYMPHATIC VESSEL
The conduit for the lymph that exits the ganglia and returns to the bloodstream

VALVE
Regulates the passage of the lymph and prevents its reflux.

VEIN

ARTERY

RETICULAR FIBERS
The networks that support the lymph nodes

B LYMPHOCYTES
acquire their immunological capacity in the bone marrow and in the liver of the fetus.

Invaders

Disequilibrium can be caused in the homeostatic mechanisms of the human body, causing disease that may or may not be infectious. Noninfectious disease is usually produced by heredity, external factors, or lifestyle. Infections are brought on by parasitic organisms, such as bacteria, viruses, fungi, and protozoa (single-celled organisms belonging to the protist kingdom).

A   BACTERIA
are found by the billions in any medium. Not all of them are harmful. Bacteria known as germs are pathogenic and release poisonous substances called toxins.

B   VIRUSES
are not really living beings but chemical packages. They consist of genetic material. When they enter the body, they invade a cell, where they reproduce and then spread.

C   PROTOZOA
are organisms that typically live in water and in soil. There are about 30 pathogenic species, which can produce a range of diseases from sleeping sickness and severe diarrhea to malaria.

LYMPHOCYTES
White blood cells that, together with the macrophages, are the basis of the cellular component of the immune system.

T CELLS
Specialized lymphocytes created in the thymus to help detect antigens

RESISTANT CAPSULE
Has the function of enveloping and protecting the ganglia

Red

THE COLOR OF INFLAMED SKIN WHEN BACTERIAL ACTION IN A WOUND CAUSES VASODILATION. THIS OCCURS BECAUSE THE BLOOD VESSELS EXPAND TO INCREASE BLOOD FLOW AS A MEANS OF DEFENSE.

Respiratory System

The respiratory system organizes and activates respiration, a process by which the human body takes in air from the atmosphere, extracts the oxygen that the circulation will bring to all the cells, and returns to the air products it does not need, such as carbon dioxide. The basic steps are inhalation, through which air enters the nose and mouth, and exhalation, through which air is expelled. Both actions are usually involuntary and automatic. Respiration involves the airway that begins in the nose and continues through the pharynx, larynx, trachea, bronchi, bronchioles, and alveoli; however, respiration occurs primarily in the two lungs, which are essentially bellows whose job it is to collect oxygen from the air. The oxygen is then distributed to the entire body via the blood. ●

WHAT ENTERS AND WHAT EXITS

Component	Percentage in Inhaled Air	Percentage of Exhaled Air
Nitrogen	78.6	78.6
Oxygen	20.8	15.6
Carbon Dioxide	0.04	4
Water Vapor	0.56	1.8
Total	**100**	**100**

Route

1. The air enters the nasal cavity, where it is heated, cleaned, and humidified (it also enters through the mouth).

2. The air passes through the pharynx, where the tonsils intercept and destroy harmful organisms.

3. The air passes through the larynx, whose upper part, the epiglottis, a cartilaginous section, prevents food from passing into the larynx when swallowing. From the larynx the air goes into the esophagus.

4. The air passes through the trachea, a tube lined with cilia and consisting of rings of cartilage that prevent its deformation. The trachea transports air to and from the lungs.

5. In the thoracic region the trachea branches into two bronchi, which are subdivided into smaller branches, the bronchioles, which in turn carry the air to the pulmonary alveoli, elastic structures shaped like sacs where gas exchange occurs.

6. From the alveoli the oxygen passes into the blood and then from the blood to the tissues of the body. The carbon dioxide exits the bloodstream and travels toward the alveoli to be subsequently exhaled. Exhaled air contains more carbon dioxide and less oxygen than inhaled air.

6 quarts (5.5 l)

THE APPROXIMATE VOLUME OF AIR THAT ENTERS AND EXITS THE LUNGS DURING ONE MINUTE OF BREATHING

15

WE NORMALLY BREATHE BETWEEN 15 AND 16 TIMES A MINUTE.

Larynx

The resonance box that houses the vocal cords; it consists of various components of cartilaginous tissue. One of these components can be identified externally: it is the Adam's apple, or thyroid cartilage, located in the middle of the throat. The larynx is important for respiration because it links the pharynx with the trachea and ensures the free passage of air entering and leaving the lungs. It closes the epiglottis like a door when the organism is ingesting food in order to prevent food from entering the airway.

HAIRS
The interior of the trachea is covered with hairs (cilia), which, like the hairs in the nose, capture dust or impurities carried by the air.

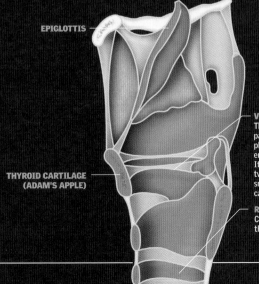

EPIGLOTTIS

THYROID CARTILAGE (ADAM'S APPLE)

VOCAL CORDS
The larynx also participates in phonation, or the emission of the voice. It does this with the two lower of the four small elastic muscles, called vocal cords.

RING
Cartilaginous ring of the trachea

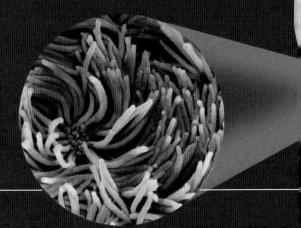

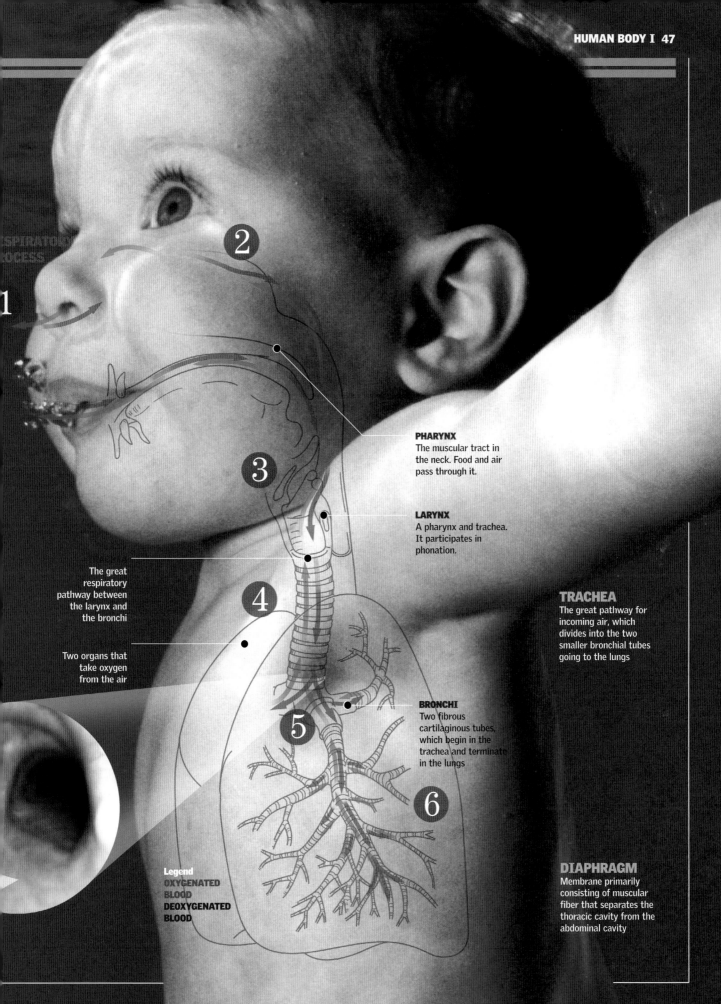

RESPIRATORY
PROCESS

1

2

3

PHARYNX
The muscular tract in
the neck. Food and air
pass through it.

LARYNX
A pharynx and trachea.
It participates in
phonation.

The great
respiratory
pathway between
the larynx and
the bronchi

4

TRACHEA
The great pathway for
incoming air, which
divides into the two
smaller bronchial tubes
going to the lungs

Two organs that
take oxygen
from the air

5

BRONCHI
Two fibrous
cartilaginous tubes,
which begin in the
trachea and terminate
in the lungs

6

Legend
OXYGENATED
BLOOD
DEOXYGENATED
BLOOD

DIAPHRAGM
Membrane primarily
consisting of muscular
fiber that separates the
thoracic cavity from the
abdominal cavity

Lungs

Their principal function is to exchange gases between the blood and the atmosphere. Inside the lungs, oxygen is taken from the air, and carbon dioxide is returned to the air. There are two lungs. The left lung has two lobes and one lingula, and it weighs approximately 30 ounces (800 g); the right lung has three lobes and weighs 35 ounces (1,000 g). Both lungs process the same amount of air. In men each lung has a capacity of 3 quarts (3.2 l), and in women, 2 quarts (2.1 l). The lungs fill most of the space in the thoracic cage surrounding the heart. Their major motions are inhalation (taking in air) and exhalation (expulsion). The pleural membranes, intercostal muscles, and diaphragm make this mobility possible. ●

Inhalation

The air enters. The diaphragm contracts and flattens. The external intercostal muscles contract, lifting the ribs upward. A space is created within the thorax into which the lungs expand. The air pressure in the lungs is less than that outside the body, and therefore air is inhaled.

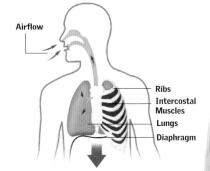

Airflow

Ribs
Intercostal
Muscles
Lungs
Diaphragm

Exhalation

The diaphragm relaxes and becomes dome-shaped. The external intercostal muscles relax. The ribs move downward and inward. The space within the thorax decreases, and the lungs are compressed. The air pressure within the lungs is greater than that outside of the body, and therefore the air is exhaled.

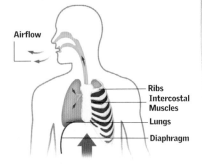

Airflow

Ribs
Intercostal
Muscles
Lungs
Diaphragm

A Marvelous Pump

➤ The respiratory system accomplishes its functions by combining a series of involuntary and automatic movements. The lungs, opening and closing like bellows, make inhalation possible by increasing their capacity to take in air, which is then exhaled when the bellows close. Inside the lungs the first stage of processing the gases that came in through the nose and the trachea is accomplished. Once the exchange of oxygen to be absorbed and carbon dioxide to be expelled occurs, the next stages can be accomplished: transport of the gases and delivery of oxygen to the cells and tissues.

30,000
THE NUMBER OF BRONCHIOLES, OR TINY BRANCHINGS OF THE BRONCHI, IN EACH LUNG

350 million
THE NUMBER OF ALVEOLI IN EACH LUNG (700 MILLION FOR BOTH TOGETHER)

PLEURAL MEMBRANES
are primarily muscular and allow the lungs to move within the rib cage.

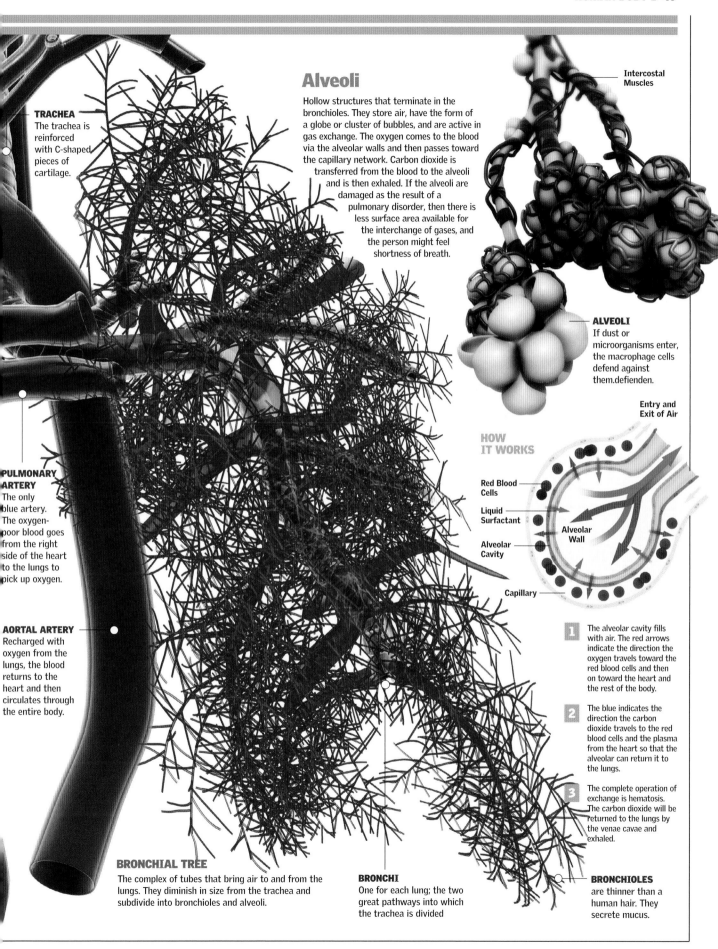

TRACHEA
The trachea is reinforced with C-shaped pieces of cartilage.

Alveoli

Hollow structures that terminate in the bronchioles. They store air, have the form of a globe or cluster of bubbles, and are active in gas exchange. The oxygen comes to the blood via the alveolar walls and then passes toward the capillary network. Carbon dioxide is transferred from the blood to the alveoli and is then exhaled. If the alveoli are damaged as the result of a pulmonary disorder, then there is less surface area available for the interchange of gases, and the person might feel shortness of breath.

Intercostal Muscles

ALVEOLI
If dust or microorganisms enter, the macrophage cells defend against them.defienden.

PULMONARY ARTERY
The only blue artery. The oxygen-poor blood goes from the right side of the heart to the lungs to pick up oxygen.

AORTAL ARTERY
Recharged with oxygen from the lungs, the blood returns to the heart and then circulates through the entire body.

Entry and Exit of Air

HOW IT WORKS

Red Blood Cells

Liquid Surfactant

Alveolar Cavity

Alveolar Wall

Capillary

1 The alveolar cavity fills with air. The red arrows indicate the direction the oxygen travels toward the red blood cells and then on toward the heart and the rest of the body.

2 The blue indicates the direction the carbon dioxide travels to the red blood cells and the plasma from the heart so that the alveolar can return it to the lungs.

3 The complete operation of exchange is hematosis. The carbon dioxide will be returned to the lungs by the venae cavae and exhaled.

BRONCHIAL TREE
The complex of tubes that bring air to and from the lungs. They diminish in size from the trachea and subdivide into bronchioles and alveoli.

BRONCHI
One for each lung; the two great pathways into which the trachea is divided

BRONCHIOLES
are thinner than a human hair. They secrete mucus.

Digestive System

The digestive system is the protagonist of a phenomenal operation that transforms food into fuel for the entire body. The process begins with ingestion through the mouth and esophagus and continues with digestion in the stomach, the small intestine, and the large intestine, from which the feces are evacuated by the rectum and anus. By then the task will have involved important chemical components, such as bile, produced by the liver, and other enzymes, produced by the pancreas, by which the food is converted into nutrients. Separating the useful from the useless requires the filtering of the kidneys, which discard the waste in urine. ●

The First Step: Ingestion

The digestive process begins with the mouth, the entry point to the large tract that changes in form and function and ends at the rectum and anus. The tongue and teeth are the first specialists in the task. The tongue is in charge of tasting and positioning the food, which is cut and ground by the teeth. This synchronized activity includes the maxillary bones, which are controlled by their corresponding muscles. The palate, in the upper part of the mouth, prevents food from passing into the nose. The natural route of the food is down the esophagus to the stomach.

Teeth

There are 32 teeth, and they are extremely hard, a condition necessary for chewing food. There are eight incisors, four canines, eight premolars, and 12 molars. Humans develop two sets of teeth, a provisional or temporary set (the baby teeth) and a permanent set (adult teeth). The first temporary teeth appear between six and 12 months of age. At 20 years of age the process of replacement that began at about age five or six is complete.

A SET OF TEETH

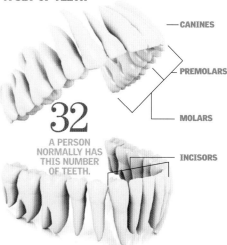

— CANINES

— PREMOLARS

— MOLARS

32
A PERSON NORMALLY HAS THIS NUMBER OF TEETH.

— INCISORS

THE MOUTH

THE SOFT PALATE
Also called the velar palate, the palate keeps the food from going into the nose.

THE HARD PALATE
The "roof" of the oral cavity. It is made of bone.

TONGUE
Its notable flexibility makes eating possible. It also tastes the food.

PHARYNX
The muscles in the walls of the pharynx contract, forcing the bolus of chewed food into the esophagus.

ESOPHAGUS
Its muscles force the bolus toward the stomach. The esophagus and stomach are separated by a sphincter.

THE INSIDE OF A TOOTH

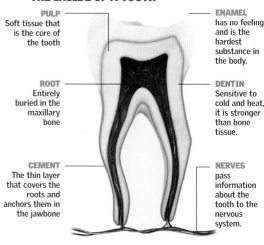

PULP
Soft tissue that is the core of the tooth

ROOT
Entirely buried in the maxillary bone

CEMENT
The thin layer that covers the roots and anchors them in the jawbone

ENAMEL
has no feeling and is the hardest substance in the body.

DENTIN
Sensitive to cold and heat, it is stronger than bone tissue.

NERVES
pass information about the tooth to the nervous system.

Enzymes and Hormones

The complex chemical processes that transform food are essentially accomplished by enzymes and hormones. Both types of substances are secreted by various glands of the digestive system, such as the salivary glands. Enzymes are substances that act as catalysts. Hormones are substances that regulate processes such as growth metabolism, reproduction, and organ function.

Digestion Chronology

The process that converts food into nutrients begins a few seconds after the food is raised to the mouth and chewing begins. The average digestion time is about 32 hours, though digestion can range from 20 to 44 hours.

Tract

The muscular movement called peristalsis pushes the food along. That is why it is possible to eat upside down or during weightlessness, as astronauts do.

1 00:00:00

The process begins when the food reaches the mouth. The entire organism is involved in the decision, but it is the digestive system that plays the main role. The first steps are taken by the teeth and the tongue, aided by the salivary glands, which provide saliva to moisten the alimentary bolus. The morsels are chewed so that they can pass through the esophagus.

2 00:00:10

About 10 seconds after chewing has begun, the food is transformed into a moist alimentary bolus that makes its way through the pharynx to the esophagus and then to the stomach, where other changes will take place.

3 03:00:00

Three hours after its arrival, the food leaves the stomach, which has accomplished its function. The first phase of digestion is over. The bolus now has a liquid and creamy consistency.

4 06:00:00

Three hours later, the food that has been digested in the stomach arrives at the midpoint of the small intestine. At this point it is ready to be absorbed.

5 08:00:00

Two hours later, the non-digested, watery residue arrives at the junction of the small and large intestines. The useless material rejected by the body's chemical selectors continues its course, and it is now prepared to be expelled from the organism in the form of feces.

20:00:00

The alimentary residue remains in the large intestine between 12 and 28 hours. In this part of the process the residue is converted into semisolid feces.

6 24:00

Between 20 and 44 hours after having entered the mouth as food, the residue that was converted into semisolid feces in the previous stage arrives at the rectum. The waste will be evacuated through the anus as excrement.

10 inches
(25 cm)
IS THE LENGTH OF
THE ESOPHAGUS.

Stomach

The part of the digestive tract that is a continuation of the esophagus. It is sometimes thought of as an expansion of the esophagus. It is the first section of the digestive system that is located in the abdomen. It has the shape of an empty bag that is curved somewhat like a bagpipe, the handle of an umbrella, or the letter "J." In the stomach, gastric juices and enzymes subject the swallowed food to intense chemical reactions while mixing it completely. The stomach connects with the duodenum through the pylorus. Peristalsis, or the muscular contractions of the alimentary canal, moves the food from the stomach to the duodenum, the next station in the progress of the alimentary bolus. ●

How We Swallow

Although swallowing is a simple act, it does require the coordination of multiple parts. The soft palate moves backward when the alimentary bolus passes through the esophagus. The epiglottis moves downward to close the trachea and prevent the food from entering the respiratory pathways. The alimentary bolus is advanced by the muscular motions of peristalsis.

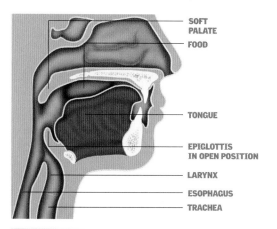

- SOFT PALATE
- FOOD
- TONGUE
- EPIGLOTTIS IN OPEN POSITION
- LARYNX
- ESOPHAGUS
- TRACHEA

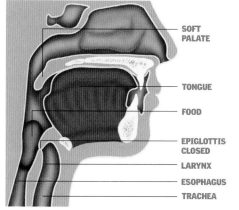

- SOFT PALATE
- TONGUE
- FOOD
- EPIGLOTTIS CLOSED
- LARYNX
- ESOPHAGUS
- TRACHEA

X-ray of the Stomach

The stomach is the best known of the internal body organs, but it is also the most misunderstood. This J-shaped sac stretches to fill up with food, but it does not absorb any of the nutrients. Its work consists of starting the digestion process, storing semi-digested food, and releasing the food slowly and continuously. Internal gastric juices make it possible for the enzymes to decompose the proteins, while muscular contractions mix the food.

PYLORUS
A muscular ring that opens and closes the pyloric sphincter to allow (or prevent) passage of liquefied food from the stomach on its way to the intestine

STOMACH WALL
A covering of three muscular layers that contract in different directions to mash the food. It contains millions of microscopic glands that secrete gastric juices.

DUODENUM
The initial section of the small intestine

20 times
THE STOMACH INCREASES UP TO 20 TIMES ITS ORIGINAL SIZE AFTER A PERSON EATS.

ESOPHAGUS
carries chewed food to
the stomach.

INFERIOR ESOPHAGEAL SPHINCTER
closes the junction between the
esophagus and the stomach to prevent
reflux of the stomach contents.

WRINKLES OR FOLDS
are formed when the stomach is
empty, but they stretch out as the
stomach fills and increases its size.

Peristalsis: Muscles in Action

Peristalsis is the group of muscular
actions that moves the food toward the
stomach and, once the digestive stage
has been completed, moves it on to the
small intestine. The sphincters are
stationary, ring-shaped muscular
structures whose opening and closing
regulates the passage of the bolus.

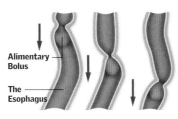

Alimentary Bolus
The Esophagus

Food is sent toward the stomach, pumped
by the muscular contractions of the
esophageal walls. Gravity helps accomplish
this downward journey.

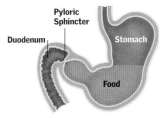

Pyloric Sphincter
Duodenum
Stomach
Food

Full stomach. Food enters. The pyloric
sphincter remains closed. The gastric juices
kill bacteria and are mixed with the food
through muscular motions.

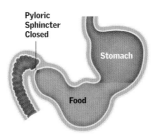

Pyloric Sphincter Closed
Stomach
Food

The stomach in full digestive action. The
peristaltic muscles mix the food until it
becomes a creamy, viscous liquid
(chyme).

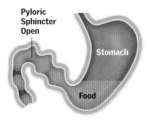

Pyloric Sphincter Open
Stomach
Food

The stomach is being emptied. The pyloric
sphincter relaxes, the muscles move the
food, and small quantities of food exit
toward the duodenum.

Stomach Wall

The structure of the wall accounts for the two
important functions of the stomach: the muscular
layers and the activity of the gastric glands
guarantee that digestion will run its course.

GASTRIC MUCOSA
contains the gastric glands, which produce
3 quarts (2.8 l) of gastric juice per day.

**MUSCULAR LAYERS OF
THE MUCOSA**
Two fine layers of
muscular fibers extend
under the mucosa.

GASTRIC WELLS
From three to seven
glands open to form a
groove.

SUBMUCOSA
Tissue that connects
the mucosa to the
layers of muscle

**THREE LAYERS
OF MUSCLE**
They are the
circular, the
longitudinal, and
the oblique.

SUBSEROSA
Layer that connects the
serosa to the muscles

SEROSA
Layer that covers the
outer surface

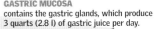

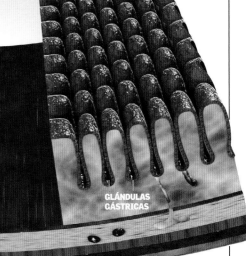

GLÁNDULAS
GÁSTRICAS

Liver, Pancreas, Bile

The liver is the largest gland of the human body and the second largest organ (the skin is the largest). It has numerous functions, and a large part of the body's general equilibrium depends on it. The liver produces bile, a yellowish-green fluid that helps in the digestion of fats. The liver is the great regulator of the glucose level of the blood, which it stores in the form of glycogen. Glycogen can be released when the organism requires more sugar for activity. The liver regulates the metabolism of proteins. Proteins are the essential chemical compounds that make up the cells of animals and plants. The liver is also a large blood filter and a storage site for vitamins A, D, E, and K. The pancreas is a gland that assists in digestion, secreting pancreatic juice. ●

Liver

Among its numerous functions, the liver rids the blood of potentially harmful chemical substances, such as drugs and germs. It filters out toxins, starting in the small intestine, and it is involved in maintaining the equilibrium of proteins, glucose, fats, cholesterol, hormones, and vitamins. The liver also participates in coagulation.

Lobules

Among its other functions, the liver processes nutrients to maintain an adequate level of glucose in the blood. This task requires hundreds of chemical processes that are carried out by the hepatocytes, or liver cells. These are arranged in columns, forming structures called lobules. They produce bile and a sterol (a solid steroid alcohol) called cholesterol. They also eliminate toxins that might be present in food.

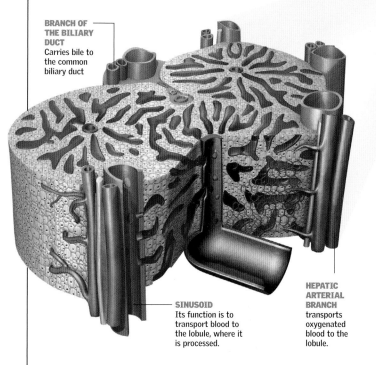

BRANCH OF THE BILIARY DUCT
Carries bile to the common biliary duct

SINUSOID
Its function is to transport blood to the lobule, where it is processed.

HEPATIC ARTERIAL BRANCH
transports oxygenated blood to the lobule.

GALLBLADDER
stores bile produced by the liver.

DUODENUM
The initial part of the small intestine

Vesicle and Bile

The biliary system stores bile that is produced by the hepatocytes in a specialized pouch called the gallbladder. The path the bile takes from the liver to the gallbladder leads through little canals, biliary ducts, and hepatic ducts, whose diameter increases as the bile moves along. When the body ingests fat, the bile is sent from the gallbladder to the small intestine to accomplish its main function: emulsifying fats to help promote their later absorption.

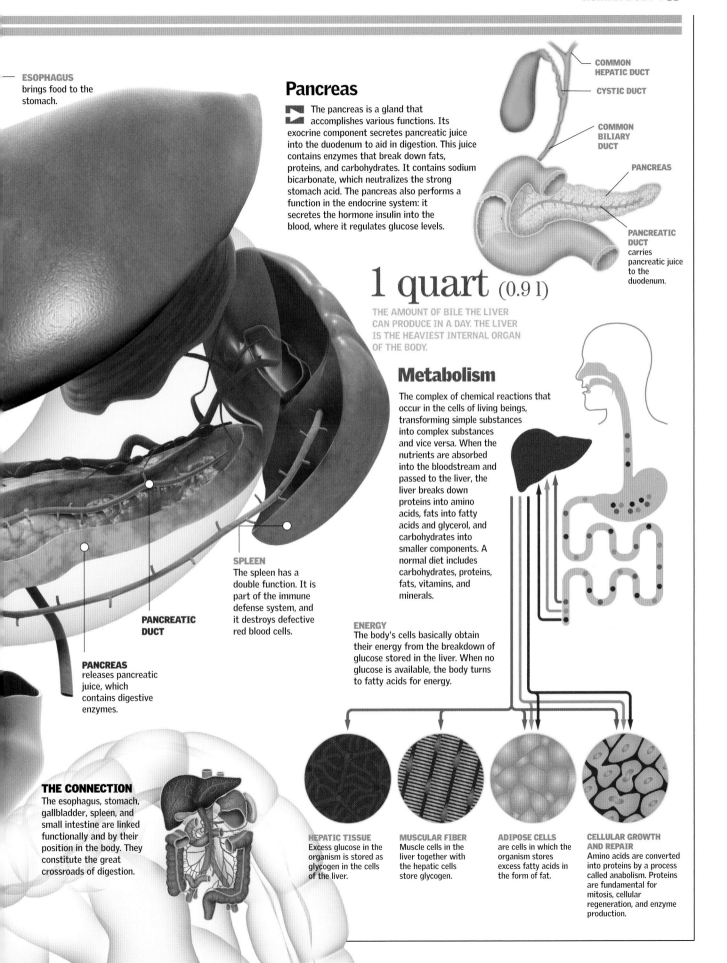

ESOPHAGUS
brings food to the stomach.

Pancreas

The pancreas is a gland that accomplishes various functions. Its exocrine component secretes pancreatic juice into the duodenum to aid in digestion. This juice contains enzymes that break down fats, proteins, and carbohydrates. It contains sodium bicarbonate, which neutralizes the strong stomach acid. The pancreas also performs a function in the endocrine system: it secretes the hormone insulin into the blood, where it regulates glucose levels.

COMMON HEPATIC DUCT

CYSTIC DUCT

COMMON BILIARY DUCT

PANCREAS

PANCREATIC DUCT
carries pancreatic juice to the duodenum.

1 quart (0.9 l)

THE AMOUNT OF BILE THE LIVER CAN PRODUCE IN A DAY. THE LIVER IS THE HEAVIEST INTERNAL ORGAN OF THE BODY.

Metabolism

The complex of chemical reactions that occur in the cells of living beings, transforming simple substances into complex substances and vice versa. When the nutrients are absorbed into the bloodstream and passed to the liver, the liver breaks down proteins into amino acids, fats into fatty acids and glycerol, and carbohydrates into smaller components. A normal diet includes carbohydrates, proteins, fats, vitamins, and minerals.

SPLEEN
The spleen has a double function. It is part of the immune defense system, and it destroys defective red blood cells.

ENERGY
The body's cells basically obtain their energy from the breakdown of glucose stored in the liver. When no glucose is available, the body turns to fatty acids for energy.

PANCREATIC DUCT

PANCREAS
releases pancreatic juice, which contains digestive enzymes.

THE CONNECTION
The esophagus, stomach, gallbladder, spleen, and small intestine are linked functionally and by their position in the body. They constitute the great crossroads of digestion.

HEPATIC TISSUE
Excess glucose in the organism is stored as glycogen in the cells of the liver.

MUSCULAR FIBER
Muscle cells in the liver together with the hepatic cells store glycogen.

ADIPOSE CELLS
are cells in which the organism stores excess fatty acids in the form of fat.

CELLULAR GROWTH AND REPAIR
Amino acids are converted into proteins by a process called anabolism. Proteins are fundamental for mitosis, cellular regeneration, and enzyme production.

Large and Small Intestine

The longest part of the digestive tract. It is about 26 to 30 feet (8 to 9 m) long and runs from the stomach to the anus. The small intestine receives the food from the stomach. Digestion continues through enzyme activity, which completes the chemical breakdown of the food. Then the definitive process of selection begins: the walls of the small intestine absorb the nutrients derived from the chemical transformation of the food. The nutrients then pass into the bloodstream. Waste substances, on the other hand, will go to the large intestine. There the final stage of the digestive process will occur: the formation of the feces to be excreted. ●

The Union of Both

The small and large intestines join at the section called the ileum (which is the final section of the small intestine; the duodenum and jejunum come before the ileum). The iliac valve acts as a door between the small intestine and large intestine, or colon. The ileum terminates in the caecum (of the large intestine). The ileum measures approximately 13 feet (4 m) in length. Its primary function is the absorption of vitamin B12 and biliary salts. The primary function of the large intestine is the absorption of water and electrolytes that arrive from the ileum.

HAUSTRUM OF THE COLON

TAENIA MUSCLE

ILEOCECAL VALVE
relaxes between meals, allowing the flow to accelerate.

ILEUM

CAECUM
Initial section of the large intestine

APPENDIX

Opening of the appendix

ASCENDING COLON
The water and mineral salts are absorbed along the length of the large intestine in a process that removes water from the digestive waste.

DUODENUM
The initial section of the small intestine, to which the secretions of the pancreas and the liver are directed

CAECUM
Initial section of the large intestine

ILEUM
Final section of the small intestine, linked with the large intestine

ANUS
Opening in the large intestine through which the feces exit

WATER THAT ENTERS THE ALIMENTARY CANAL		
In fluid ounces		
Saliva	34	(1 l)
Water from Drinking	77	(2.3 l)
Bile	34	(1 l)
Pancreatic Juice	68	(2 l)
Gastric Juice	68	(2 l)
Intestinal Juice	34	(1 l)
Total	**313**	**(9.3 l)**

WATER REABSORBED BY THE ALIMENTARY CANAL		
In fluid ounces		
Small Intestine	280	(8.3 l)
Large Intestine	30	(0.9 l)
Subtotal	310	(9.2 l)
Water Lost in the Feces	3	(0.1 l)
Total	**313**	**(9.3 l)**

Differences and Similarities

The small intestine is longer than the large intestine. The length of the small intestine is between 20 and 23 feet (between 6 and 7 m), and the large intestine averages 5 feet (1.5 m). Their respective composition and functions are complementary.

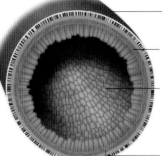

LARGE INTESTINE

SEROSA
The external protective membrane in both

SUBMUCOSA
In both, the loose covering with vessels and nerves

MUCOSA
It is thin and absorbs nutrients via projections or hairs.
Absorbent fat that excretes mucus.

MUSCULAR
Thin muscle fibers that are longitudinal externally and circular internally. The fibers are also covered with hairs, maximizing the area of the mucosa.
Fatty rigid layer that mixes and pushes the feces

SMALL INTESTINE

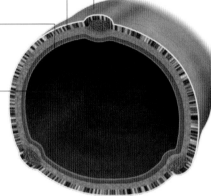

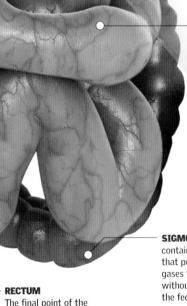

TRANSVERSE COLON
The undigested remains begin to be transformed into feces.

DESCENDING COLON
The feces are solidified and accumulate before being expelled.

JEJUNUM
The intermediate part of the small intestine, which links the duodenum with the ileum

SIGMOID COLON
contains a structure that permits the gases to pass without pushing the feces.

RECTUM
The final point of the accumulation of the feces. Its storage capacity is small.

Villa

The internal wall of the small intestine is covered with millions of hairlike structures called villi. Each one has a lymphatic vessel and a network of vessels that deliver nutrients to it. Each villus is covered by a cellular layer that absorbs nutrients. Together with epithelial cells, the villi function to increase the surface area of the intestine and optimize the absorption of nutrients.

VILLA

LYMPHATIC CAPILLARY

ARTERIAL CAPILLARY

VENOUS CAPILLARY

MUCOSA

SUBMUCOSA

TUNICA MUSCULARIS

Urinary System

I ts basic organs are the kidneys (2), the ureters (2), the bladder, and the urethra. Its function is to regulate homeostasis, maintaining the equilibrium between the water and the chemicals in the body. The first phase of this objective is accomplished when the kidneys produce and secrete urine, a liquid that is eliminated from the body. Urine is essentially harmless, only containing about 2 percent urea, and is sterile: it is composed primarily of water and salts, and it normally does not contain bacteria, viruses, or fungi. The ureters are channels that carry the urine through the body. The bladder is a sac that stores the urine until it is passed to the urethra, a duct through which it will be expelled from the body. ●

The Urinary Tract

The glomerulus is a grouping of vessels located in the cortex of the kidneys. Most of the filtering that takes place in the nephron is performed in the glomerulus. Wide arterioles carry blood to the glomerulus. Other, thinner arterioles exit from the glomerulus, carrying away blood. So much pressure is generated inside the kidney that the fluid exits from the blood via the porous capillary walls.

The Bladder in Action

The bladder is continually filled with urine and then emptied periodically. When full, the bladder stretches to increase its capacity. When the muscle of the internal sphincter is relaxed, the muscles of the wall contract, and the urine exits through the urethra. In adults this occurs voluntarily in response to an order issued by the nervous system. In infants, on the other hand, this evacuation occurs spontaneously, as soon as the bladder is filled.

FILLING

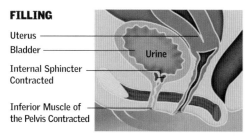

Uterus
Bladder
Urine
Internal Sphincter Contracted
Inferior Muscle of the Pelvis Contracted

EMPTYING

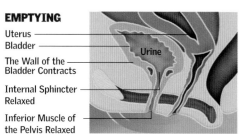

Uterus
Bladder
Urine
The Wall of the Bladder Contracts
Internal Sphincter Relaxed
Inferior Muscle of the Pelvis Relaxed

Legend

1. BLOOD FILTERING
The blood enters the kidney via the renal artery.

2. TRANSFER
The artery carries the blood into the kidney, where it is filtered by the kidney's functional units, the nephrons.

3. STORAGE
A certain amount of urine is obtained from the filtrate in the nephrons, and that urine is sent to the renal pelvis.

4. ELIMINATION
The urine passes from the renal pelvis to the ureter and then to the bladder, where it accumulates until it is eliminated through the tube-shaped urethra.

15 minutes

IT TAKES 15 MINUTES FOR LIQUIDS TO CIRCULATE THROUGH THE NEPHRONS.

COMPONENTS OF URINE

95%	**Water**
2%	**Urea,** a toxic substance
2%	**Chloride salts,** sulfates, phosphates of potassium and magnesium
1%	**Uric acid**

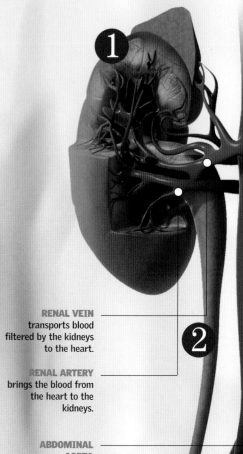

RENAL VEIN transports blood filtered by the kidneys to the heart.

RENAL ARTERY brings the blood from the heart to the kidneys.

ABDOMINAL AORTA A section of the large circulatory canal. It provides blood to the renal artery.

BLADDER A hollow organ with a fatty muscle wall in which urine is temporarily stored

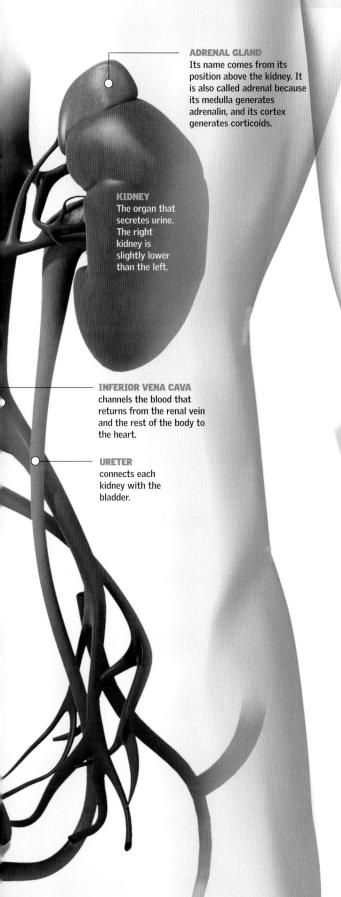

ADRENAL GLAND
Its name comes from its position above the kidney. It is also called adrenal because its medulla generates adrenalin, and its cortex generates corticoids.

KIDNEY
The organ that secretes urine. The right kidney is slightly lower than the left.

INFERIOR VENA CAVA
channels the blood that returns from the renal vein and the rest of the body to the heart.

URETER
connects each kidney with the bladder.

Differences by Sex

The urinary system has a double relationship to the reproductive system. The two systems are linked by their close physical proximity, but they are also linked functionally. For example, the ureter is a vehicle for secretions produced by the glands of both systems. The urinary systems in men and women are different. A man's bladder is larger, and the male ureter is also larger than a woman's, because in a man the ureter extends to the end of the penis, for a total length of about 6 inches (20 cm); in a woman, on the other hand, the bladder is located at the front of the uterus, and the length of the ureter is approximately 1.5 inches (4 cm).

IN A MAN

IN A WOMAN

KIDNEY

URETER

BLADDER

UTERUS

URETER

PROSTATE

PENIS

TESTICLE

VAGINAL OPENING

Fluid Exchange

The volume of urine that a person expels every day is related to the person's consumption of liquids. Three quarts (2.5 l) a day would be excessive, but a significant decrease in the production of urine can indicate a problem. The table details the relationship between the consumption of liquid and its expulsion by the different glands of the human body.

CONSUMPTION OF WATER	
Drinking	**60%**
50 fluid ounces (1,500 ml)	
Food	**30%**
25 fluid ounces (750 ml)	
Metabolic water	**10%**
16 fluid ounces (250 ml)	
3 quarts (2,500 ml) TOTAL	

EXPULSIÓN DE AGUA	
Urine	**60%**
50 fluid ounces (1,500 ml)	
Losses through the lungs and the skin	**28%**
25 fluid ounces (700 ml)	
Sweat	**8%**
16 fluid ounces (200 ml)	
Feces	**4%**
3 fluid ounces (100 ml)	
3 quarts (2,500 ml) TOTAL	

Kidneys

Located on either side of the spinal column, the kidneys are the fundamental organs of the urinary system. They regulate the amount of water and minerals in the blood by producing urine that carries away the waste the kidneys discard. They keep the composition of the bodily fluids constant, regulate the pressure of the arteries, and produce important substances such as the precursor of vitamin D and erythropoietin. Every day they process 500 gallons (1,750 l) of blood and produce 2 quarts (1.5 l) of urine. The kidneys measure approximately 5 inches (12 cm) long and 3 inches (6 cm) wide. Their weight is only 1 percent of the total body weight, but they consume 25 percent of its energy. If one kidney ceases to function, the body is able to survive with the activity of the other. ●

RENAL PYRAMID
A fluted structure in the form of a pyramid, located in the renal medulla

The Renal Circuit

Urine is produced in the nephrons in each kidney; there are thought to be a million nephrons in each kidney. From the nephrons the urine flows into the proximal convoluted tubule, where all the nutrients, such as glucose, amino acids, and most of the water and salts, are reabsorbed into the blood. After passing through the nephron the urine is filtered, and it arrives at the common collecting duct where only the residues and excess water are retained.

RENAL PELVIS
transports the urine to the ureter.

2 **3**

1. ENTRY OF BLOOD
The blood enters the kidney via the renal artery.

2. FILTRATION
The blood is filtered in the nephrons, the functional units of the kidneys.

3. URINE IS OBTAINED
A certain amount of urine is obtained from the filtrate in the nephrons, and it is sent to the renal pelvis. The filtered blood, free from waste, is sent to the renal vein and reenters the bloodstream.

4. URINE
The urine passes through the renal pelvis to the ureter and from there to the bladder, where it accumulates until it is eliminated through the tube-shaped urethra.

5. CLEAN BLOOD
The clean blood exits the kidney via the renal vein, which is connected to the vena cava. The blood then returns to the heart.

45 minutes

THE FRENCH PHYSIOLOGIST CLAUDE BERNARD (1813-78) WAS THE FIRST TO NOTE THE IMPORTANCE OF THE KIDNEYS.

At that time it was not known that the kidneys filter all the water content of the blood in the body every 45 minutes and that, even so, it is possible to survive with only one kidney (or none, in the case of dialysis).

RENAL CAPSULE
Protective layer that covers each kidney. It consists of white fibrous tissue.

1 million
ONE KIDNEY HAS ABOUT ONE MILLION NEPHRONS.

41 to 51
fluid ounces
(1,200 to 1,500 cc)
IS THE AMOUNT OF URINE ELIMINATED EACH DAY BY AN ADULT.

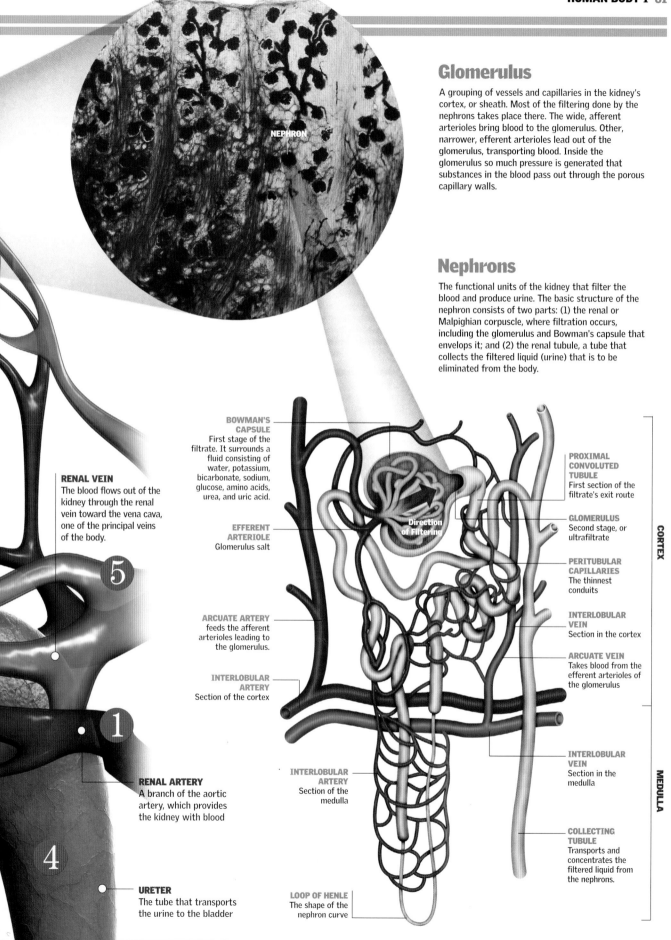

NEPHRON

Glomerulus

A grouping of vessels and capillaries in the kidney's cortex, or sheath. Most of the filtering done by the nephrons takes place there. The wide, afferent arterioles bring blood to the glomerulus. Other, narrower, efferent arterioles lead out of the glomerulus, transporting blood. Inside the glomerulus so much pressure is generated that substances in the blood pass out through the porous capillary walls.

Nephrons

The functional units of the kidney that filter the blood and produce urine. The basic structure of the nephron consists of two parts: (1) the renal or Malpighian corpuscle, where filtration occurs, including the glomerulus and Bowman's capsule that envelops it; and (2) the renal tubule, a tube that collects the filtered liquid (urine) that is to be eliminated from the body.

RENAL VEIN
The blood flows out of the kidney through the renal vein toward the vena cava, one of the principal veins of the body.

5

1

RENAL ARTERY
A branch of the aortic artery, which provides the kidney with blood

4

URETER
The tube that transports the urine to the bladder

BOWMAN'S CAPSULE
First stage of the filtrate. It surrounds a fluid consisting of water, potassium, bicarbonate, sodium, glucose, amino acids, urea, and uric acid.

EFFERENT ARTERIOLE
Glomerulus salt

ARCUATE ARTERY
feeds the afferent arterioles leading to the glomerulus.

INTERLOBULAR ARTERY
Section of the cortex

INTERLOBULAR ARTERY
Section of the medulla

LOOP OF HENLE
The shape of the nephron curve

Direction of Filtering

PROXIMAL CONVOLUTED TUBULE
First section of the filtrate's exit route

GLOMERULUS
Second stage, or ultrafiltrate

PERITUBULAR CAPILLARIES
The thinnest conduits

INTERLOBULAR VEIN
Section in the cortex

ARCUATE VEIN
Takes blood from the efferent arterioles of the glomerulus

INTERLOBULAR VEIN
Section in the medulla

COLLECTING TUBULE
Transports and concentrates the filtered liquid from the nephrons.

CORTEX

MEDULLA

Endocrine System

C onsists of the glands inside the body that secrete approximately 50 specific substances called hormones into the blood. The hormones activate or stimulate various organs and control reproduction, development, and metabolism. These chemicals control many of the body's processes and even meddle in our love lives. ●

The Hormonal Message

The endocrine system is made up of the so-called endocrine glands. This complex, controlled by the pituitary (hypophysis), or master, gland, includes the thyroid, parathyroid, pancreas, ovaries, testicles, adrenals, pineal, and hypothalamus. The role of these glands is to secrete the many hormones needed for body functions. The word "hormone" comes from the Greek *hormon*, which means to excite or incite. The term was suggested in 1905 by the British physiologist Ernest Starling, who in 1902 assisted in the isolation of the first hormone, secretin, which stimulates intestinal activity. Hormones control such functions as reproduction, metabolism (digestion and elimination of food), and the body's growth and development. However, by controlling an organism's energy and nutritional levels, they also affect its responses to the environment.

Pituitary Hormones

ACTH Adrenocorticotropin hormone. It goes to the adrenal gland.

TSH A hormone that stimulates the thyroid to produce the thyroid hormones, which influence metabolism, energy, and the nervous system.

GH Growth hormone

FSH Follicle-stimulating hormone

LH Luteinizing hormone; testosterone and estrogen

MSH Hormone that stimulates the melanocyte of the skin.

ADH Antidiuretic hormone

PRL Prolactin; stimulates milk production by the mother.

OXYTOCIN Stimulates the release of milk by the mother, as well as the contractions needed during labor.

The Master Gland

The pituitary gland, or hypophysis, is also called the master gland because it controls the rest of the endocrine glands. It is divided into two parts, the anterior lobe and the posterior lobe. The pituitary hormones stimulate the other glands to generate specific hormones needed by the organism.

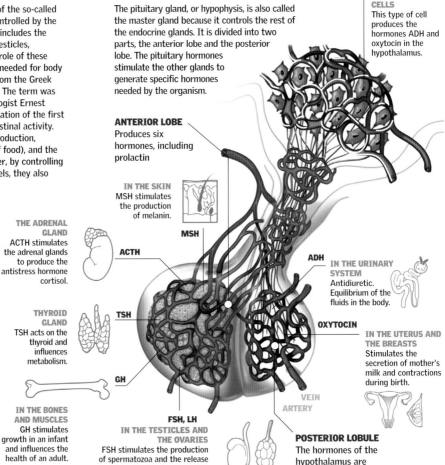

NEUROSECRETORY CELLS
This type of cell produces the hormones ADH and oxytocin in the hypothalamus.

ANTERIOR LOBE
Produces six hormones, including prolactin

IN THE SKIN
MSH stimulates the production of melanin.

MSH

ACTH

THE ADRENAL GLAND
ACTH stimulates the adrenal glands to produce the antistress hormone cortisol.

THYROID GLAND
TSH acts on the thyroid and influences metabolism.

TSH

ADH

IN THE URINARY SYSTEM
Antidiuretic. Equilibrium of the fluids in the body.

OXYTOCIN

IN THE UTERUS AND THE BREASTS
Stimulates the secretion of mother's milk and contractions during birth.

GH

IN THE BONES AND MUSCLES
GH stimulates growth in an infant and influences the health of an adult.

VEIN
ARTERY

FSH, LH
IN THE TESTICLES AND THE OVARIES
FSH stimulates the production of spermatozoa and the release of ovules. LH also generates testosterone.

POSTERIOR LOBULE
The hormones of the hypothalamus are stored here.

The Confidence Hormone

Oxytocin, the hormone that influences basic functions, such as being in love, orgasm, birth, and breast-feeding, is associated with affection and tenderness. It is a hormone that stimulates the formation of bonds of affection.

A Kiss

Kissing is considered to be healthy because, among other things, it stimulates the production of numerous hormones and chemical substances.

PHEROMONES
are chemical substances released by the glands distributed in the skin that are related to sexual attraction. They act like hormones (whether or not they are actually hormones is a matter of dispute). They transmit sensations of attraction, excitation, and rejection.

PITUITARY GLAND OR HYPOPHYSIS:
The pituitary gland is located at the base of the brain, and it is the most important control center of the endocrine system. It releases oxytocin in anticipation of a kiss; it is the hormone that stimulates orgasm, birth, and breast-feeding; and it is also associated with psychological behaviors such as affection and tenderness.

PINEAL

PARATHYROID

THYROID

MAMMARY GLANDS
The LH hormone excites the production of estrogen hormones, which regulate female sexuality; the activity of the mammary glands; and the menstrual cycle. Puberty is marked by an increase of estrogen production.

ADRENAL GLANDS
The hormone adrenaline "awakens" the body before a risk—or before a kiss. It increases the cardiac rhythm, the arterial pressure, the level of glucose in the blood, and the flow of blood to muscles.

PANCREAS
Before a kiss, it increases the glucose level in the blood. The pancreas produces the two hormones that control the blood sugar level: insulin and glycogen.

SEXUAL GLANDS
The reproductive system responds to the same pituitary hormones in men and women: luteinizing hormone (LH) and follicle-stimulating hormone (FSH). (Both are released and activated in anticipation of a kiss.)

Male Reproductive System

The male reproductive system is the complex of organs that leads to a man's production of one of two types of cells necessary for the creation of a new being. The principal organs are the two testicles, or male gonads, and the penis. The testicles serve as a factory for the production of millions of cells called spermatozoa, which are minute messengers of conception bearing the genetic information for the fertilization of the ovum. The penis is linked to the urinary apparatus, but for reproduction it is the organ that functions as a vehicle for semen, a liquid through which the spermatozoa can reach their destination. The word "semen" comes from Greek and means "seed." ●

Testicles and Spermatozoa

The seminiferous tubes in the testicles are covered with spermatogenic cells. By a process of successive cellular divisions called meiosis, the spermatogenic cells are transformed into spermatozoa, the term for the gametes, or male sexual cells, the bearers of half of the genetic information of a new individual. The spermatozoa fertilize the ovum, or female gamete, which contains the other half of the genetic information. The number of chromosomes is kept constant because the spermatozoa and the ovum are both haploid cells (cells that possess half of the genetic information of other cells). When the two haploid cells unite, the fertilized egg, or zygote, is a diploid cell (which contains a total of 46 chromosomes).

THE TESTICLES
The sexual organs that produce sperm

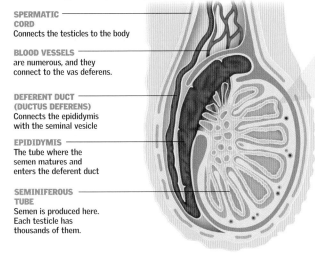

SPERMATIC CORD
Connects the testicles to the body

BLOOD VESSELS
are numerous, and they connect to the vas deferens.

DEFERENT DUCT (DUCTUS DEFERENS)
Connects the epididymis with the seminal vesicle

EPIDIDYMIS
The tube where the semen matures and enters the deferent duct

SEMINIFEROUS TUBE
Semen is produced here. Each testicle has thousands of them.

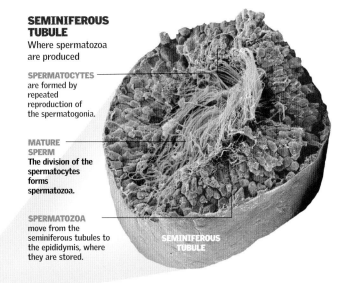

SEMINIFEROUS TUBULE
Where spermatozoa are produced

SPERMATOCYTES
are formed by repeated reproduction of the spermatogonia.

MATURE SPERM
The division of the spermatocytes forms spermatozoa.

SPERMATOZOA
move from the seminiferous tubules to the epididymis, where they are stored.

SEMINIFEROUS TUBULE

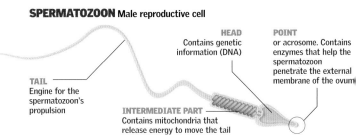

SPERMATOZOON Male reproductive cell

HEAD
Contains genetic information (DNA)

POINT
or acrosome. Contains enzymes that help the spermatozoon penetrate the external membrane of the ovum

TAIL
Engine for the spermatozoon's propulsion

INTERMEDIATE PART
Contains mitochondria that release energy to move the tail

Internal Structure of the Penis

The most characteristic organ of a man's body, the penis has a cylindrical form with a double function for the urinary system and the reproductive system. In its normal, or relaxed, state the penis carries urine from the body via the urethra during urination. In its erect state its rigidity permits it to be introduced into the female vagina and to release sperm through ejaculation. The penis consists of spongy tissue supplied with blood vessels. The circulatory system supplies abundant blood to these vessels during sexual arousal so that the spongy tissue becomes swollen because of the filled blood vessels. This produces an erection, which makes copulation possible. The body of the penis surrounds the urethra and is connected to the pubic bone. The prepuce covers the head (glans) of the penis, which is located above the scrotum.

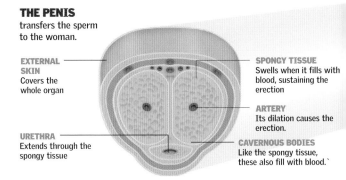

THE PENIS
transfers the sperm to the woman.

EXTERNAL SKIN
Covers the whole organ

SPONGY TISSUE
Swells when it fills with blood, sustaining the erection

ARTERY
Its dilation causes the erection.

URETHRA
Extends through the spongy tissue

CAVERNOUS BODIES
Like the spongy tissue, these also fill with blood.`

Prostate and Epididymis

The prostate is a gland located in front of the rectum and below the bladder. It is the size of a walnut, and it surrounds the urethra, a tube that carries urine from the bladder. The prostate produces the liquid for the semen, which carries the spermatozoa. During orgasm, muscular contractions occur that send the liquid from the prostate out through the urethra. The epididymis is a duct that, when stretched out to its full length, is approximately 20 feet (5 m) long. In the male body it is extremely coiled and lies on the back surface of the testicles, where it is connected with the corresponding vas deferens. The vas deferens stores spermatozoa and provides them with an exit route. The seminal vesicles are two membranous receptacles that connect to both sides of the vas deferens and form the ejaculatory duct.

150 million

THE NUMBER OF SPERMATOZOA THAT EACH 0.06 CUBIC INCH (1 ML) OF SEMEN CAN CONTAIN

THE GLANDS

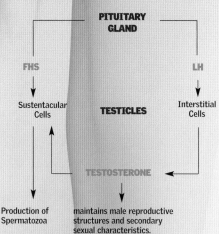

PITUITARY GLAND

FHS

LH

Sustentacular Cells

TESTICLES

Interstitial Cells

TESTOSTERONE

Production of Spermatozoa

maintains male reproductive structures and secondary sexual characteristics.

93° F
(34° C)

IS THE IDEAL APPROXIMATE TEMPERATURE REQUIRED BY THE TESTICLES TO PRODUCE SEMEN.
It is lower than the normal body temperature of 98.6° F (37° C) because that temperature would be too warm for this function. This explains why the testicles are outside of the body. Depending on the ambient temperature, they extend or retract.

BLADDER
Receptacle of the urinary system that temporarily stores urine

PROSTATE
Gland that secretes a creamy liquid (semen) along with the ejaculated sperm

EJACULATORY DUCT
A short tube that carries the sperm to the urethra

SEMINAL VESICLE
Secretes fluid and assorted nutrients into the sperm during ejaculation

PREPUCE
Covers and protects the head of the penis

GLANS
Extremity of the penis

TESTICLE
Gland that produces sperm

SCROTUM
Sac of skin that contains the testicles

EPIDIDYMIS
Spiral tube where the sperm matures

Female Reproductive System

I ts primary function is the production of ova, and its organs are arranged so as to allow the fertilization of the ovum by a spermatozoon of the male reproductive system and from that moment to facilitate a series of processes known collectively as pregnancy for the creation of a new being. The internal organs of the female reproductive system are the vagina, the uterus, the ovaries, and the fallopian tubes. The external genitalia, generally referred to as the vulva, are relatively hidden and include the labia majora and minora, the clitoris, the urinary meatus, Bartholin's glands, and the vaginal orifice that leads to the vagina. The menstrual cycle governs the system's function. ●

The 28 Days of the Menstrual Cycle

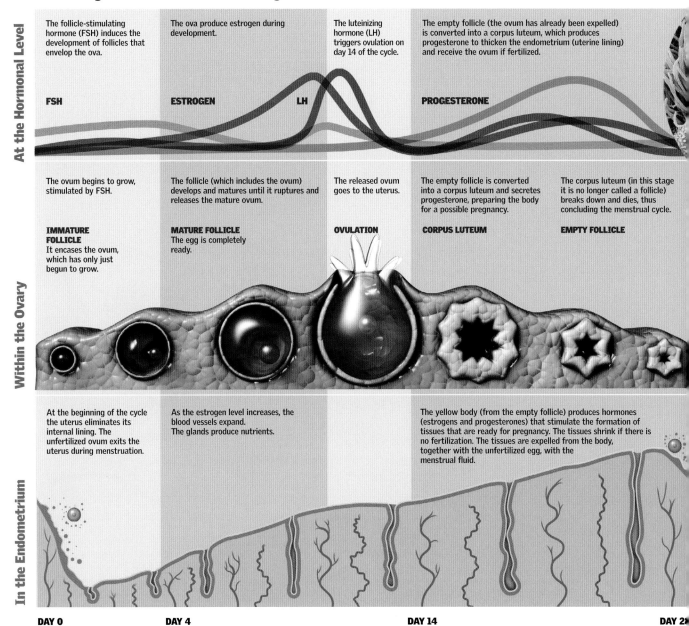

At the Hormonal Level

The follicle-stimulating hormone (FSH) induces the development of follicles that envelop the ova.

The ova produce estrogen during development.

The luteinizing hormone (LH) triggers ovulation on day 14 of the cycle.

The empty follicle (the ovum has already been expelled) is converted into a corpus luteum, which produces progesterone to thicken the endometrium (uterine lining) and receive the ovum if fertilized.

FSH **ESTROGEN** **LH** **PROGESTERONE**

Within the Ovary

The ovum begins to grow, stimulated by FSH.

The follicle (which includes the ovum) develops and matures until it ruptures and releases the mature ovum.

The released ovum goes to the uterus.

The empty follicle is converted into a corpus luteum and secretes progesterone, preparing the body for a possible pregnancy.

The corpus luteum (in this stage it is no longer called a follicle) breaks down and dies, thus concluding the menstrual cycle.

IMMATURE FOLLICLE
It encases the ovum, which has only just begun to grow.

MATURE FOLLICLE
The egg is completely ready.

OVULATION

CORPUS LUTEUM

EMPTY FOLLICLE

In the Endometrium

At the beginning of the cycle the uterus eliminates its internal lining. The unfertilized ovum exits the uterus during menstruation.

As the estrogen level increases, the blood vessels expand. The glands produce nutrients.

The yellow body (from the empty follicle) produces hormones (estrogens and progesterones) that stimulate the formation of tissues that are ready for pregnancy. The tissues shrink if there is no fertilization. The tissues are expelled from the body, together with the unfertilized egg, with the menstrual fluid.

DAY 0 **DAY 4** **DAY 14** **DAY 28**

2 million

IS THE APPROXIMATE NUMBER OF OVA THAT AN INFANT GIRL HAS IN HER BODY AT BIRTH. BETWEEN THE AGES OF 10 AND 14, ABOUT 300,000 TO 400,000 OVA REMAIN, OF WHICH ONLY 400 WILL MATURE COMPLETELY OVER HER LIFETIME.

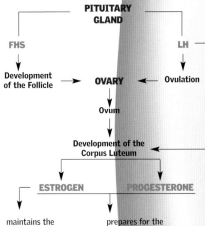

Cilia, tiny hairlike structures, move the ova very smoothly.

Menstruation: The Key to Female Reproduction

The female reproductive system is more protected than that of the male because the bony structure of the pelvis houses and shields it. Its development begins around the age of 10, when the female hormones begin a three- to four-year process during which the genital organs, the breasts, the pubic hair, and the general shape of the body change. Toward the age of 13, sometimes earlier or later, the first menstruation, called the menarche, occurs, signaling the beginning of a woman's fertility. She will normally remain fertile for several decades. During menopause, when fertilization is no longer possible, a woman's sexual life is usually not affected and can continue normally.

FALLOPIAN TUBE
A tube close to each ovary that receives the mature ovum and transports it to the uterus. It measures 4 inches (10 cm) long and 0.1 inch (0.3 cm) in diameter.

FIMBRIAE
Filamentary formations that guide the released ovum toward the fallopian tube during ovulation

OVARY
Contains follicles of the ova, one of which matures during each menstrual cycle

UTERUS
The muscular walls stretch to accommodate the fetus during its development.

CERVIX
The neck of the uterus through which the menstrual fluid and other secretions pass. It allows the sperm to enter and the fluid from the menstrual cycle to exit. It greatly expands during birth.

VAGINA
An elastic muscular tube that stretches during sexual relations and birth; it has an internal mucous membrane that provides lubrication and an acid medium that acts as a defense against infection. It serves as the pathway of the uterus to the exterior.

CLITORIS
A sensitive protuberance of tissue that responds to sexual stimulation

THE GLANDS

PITUITARY GLAND

FHS → Development of the Follicle → **OVARY** ← Ovulation ← LH

OVARY → Ovum → Development of the Corpus Luteum

Development of the Corpus Luteum → ESTROGEN, PROGESTERONE

ESTROGEN
maintains the reproductive structures and secondary sexual characteristics.

PROGESTERONE
prepares for the implementation and control of the menstrual cycle.

The Senses and Speech

Everything we know about the world comes to us through the senses. Traditionally it was thought that we had only five: vision, hearing, touch, smell, and taste. However, for some time now we have known that we have many additional classes of sensations—such as pain, pressure, temperature, muscular sensation, and a sense of

HEALTHY AND SHINY SKIN
The health of the skin
depends upon a diet that
provides the organism with a
sufficient amount of proteins
and minerals.

SMELL AND TASTE 70-71

TOUCH AND THE SKIN 72-73

ANATOMY OF THE EYE 74-75

THE MECHANICS OF HEARING 76-77

SPEECH AND NONVERBAL LANGUAGE 78-79

motion—that are generally included in the sense of touch. The areas of the brain involved are called somatosensory areas. Although we often take our senses for granted, each one of them is delicate and irreplaceable. Without them it is nearly impossible to understand our surroundings. They are a bridge between us and everything alive on the Earth. ●

Smell and Taste

These two senses of the body function as powerful allies of the digestive system. Taste involves the perception of dissolved chemical substances arriving, for example, in the form of food. Taste sensation is principally seated on the upper surface of the tongue, and saliva is a fundamental ingredient for dissolving and tasting. Smell involves the perception of these chemicals when they take the form of dispersed aromas. The sense of smell operates at a greater distance than that of taste and can capture substances floating in the environment. It is thought that smell is some 10,000 times more sensitive than any of our other senses. ●

Olfactory Cells

These are located deep in the nasal cavity, extended over the so-called olfactory epithelium. It is calculated that some 25 million cells are located there. Their useful life is, on average, 30 days, after which they are replaced by new cells. They have a dual function. One end of each olfactory receptor is connected to the olfactory bulb and transmits the sensations it records, so that the bulb is able to send the nerve impulses to the brain with the necessary information. The other end terminates in a group of cilia, or microscopic hairs, which serve a protective function within the mucosa.

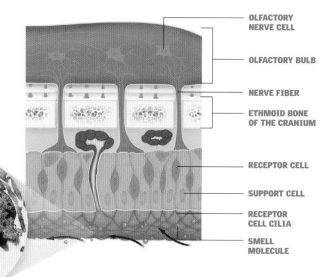

OLFACTORY NERVE CELL

OLFACTORY BULB

NERVE FIBER

ETHMOID BONE OF THE CRANIUM

RECEPTOR CELL

SUPPORT CELL

RECEPTOR CELL CILIA

SMELL MOLECULE

10,000
THE NUMBER OF ODORS THE SENSE OF SMELL CAN DISTINGUISH

Gustatory Papillae

The tongue is the principal seat of the sense of taste. It has great mobility at the bottom of the mouth and contains between 5,000 and 12,000 gustatory papillae. Each of these papillae has approximately 50 sensory cells, which have an average life span of 10 days. The salivary glands are activated by the ingestion of food or just before ingestion. They generate an alkaline liquid called saliva, a chemical solvent that, together with the tongue, breaks down the substances of which food is composed and makes it possible to differentiate between them by taste. The tongue takes charge of perceiving these tastes via the fungiform papillae, which give the tongue its rough appearance.

4 Flavors
THE SURFACE OF THE TONGUE CAN DISTINGUISH: SWEET, SALTY, SOUR, AND BITTER.

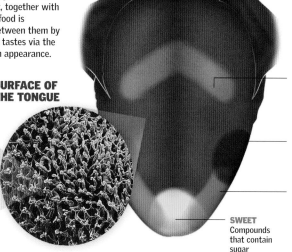

GUSTATORY PAPILLA

TASTE PORE

TASTE HAIRS

CELL RECEPTOR

SUPPORT CELL

SURFACE OF THE TONGUE

BITTER
A disagreeable and enduring sensation

SOUR
Produces acidity

SALTY
Contains more salt than necessary

SWEET
Compounds that contain sugar

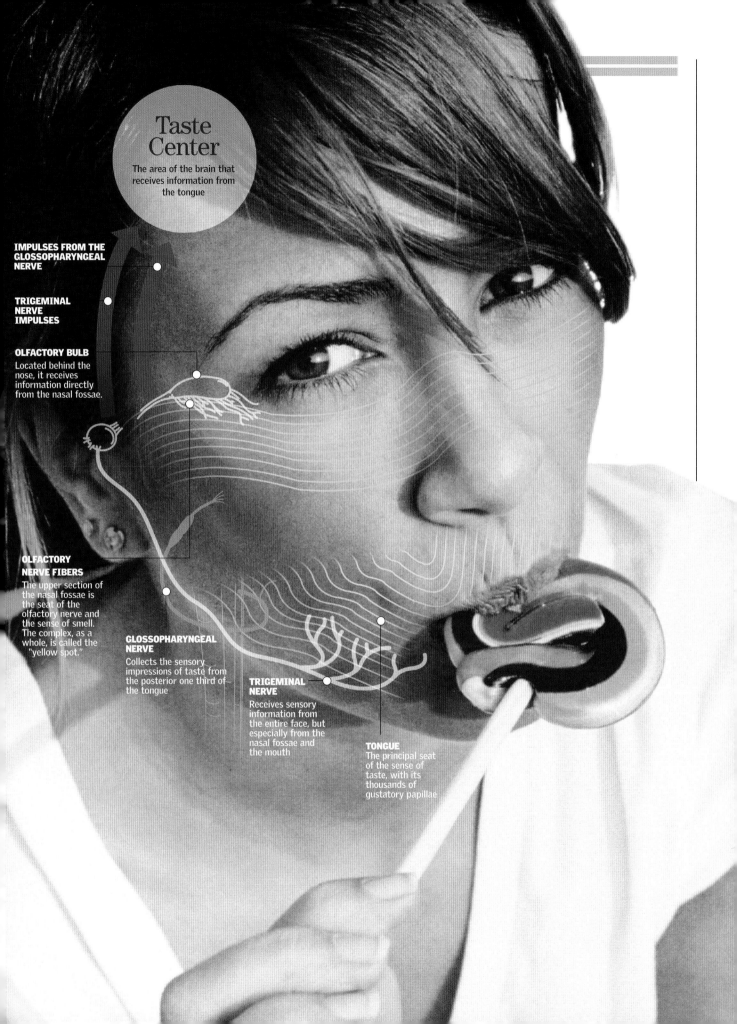

Taste Center

The area of the brain that receives information from the tongue

IMPULSES FROM THE GLOSSOPHARYNGEAL NERVE

TRIGEMINAL NERVE IMPULSES

OLFACTORY BULB
Located behind the nose, it receives information directly from the nasal fossae.

OLFACTORY NERVE FIBERS
The upper section of the nasal fossae is the seat of the olfactory nerve and the sense of smell. The complex, as a whole, is called the "yellow spot."

GLOSSOPHARYNGEAL NERVE
Collects the sensory impressions of taste from the posterior one third of the tongue

TRIGEMINAL NERVE
Receives sensory information from the entire face, but especially from the nasal fossae and the mouth

TONGUE
The principal seat of the sense of taste, with its thousands of gustatory papillae

Touch and the Skin

Touch is one of the five senses. Its function is to perceive sensations of contact, pressure, and temperature and to send them to the brain. It is located in the skin (the integument), the organ that covers the entire outside of the body for protection. The cellular renewal of the skin is continuous, and when recording external changes (of temperature, for example), it activates reflexive mechanisms to open or close the pores and, thus, to maintain the required body temperature. Secretions, such as those of the sweat glands, also contribute to this process by reducing heat. Like the sebaceous glands, they are important for hydration and hygiene in the areas where they are located. ●

The Thinnest and the Thickest

■◣ The thinnest skin on the body is that of the eyelids. The thickest is that of the sole of the foot. Both provide, like all the skin of the body, a protective function for muscles, bones, nerves, blood vessels, and interior organs. It is thought that hair and fingernails are modified types of skin. Hair grows over the whole body, except for the palms of the hands, the soles of the feet, the eyelids, and the lips.

MERKEL DISK
or Merkel cell. It is specialized to detect pressure. They are located in the palms of the hand and the soles of the feet.

RUFFINI CORPUSCLE
Capsules deep in the skin and the ligaments; stretch receptors

VENULAE
Small blood vessels. When they break, because of a blow for example, hematomas appear.

UPPER SQUAMOUS LAYER
or hornlike layer. It is superficial, granulated, and transparent.

EPIDERMIS
Impermeable to water. It is external and is the thinnest layer. It is wear-resistant.

DERMIS
The middle layer, which is below the epidermis and is thicker

SUBCUTANEOUS FAT
Also called the hypodermis. It is an energy reservoir that acts as a thermal insulator and cushion.

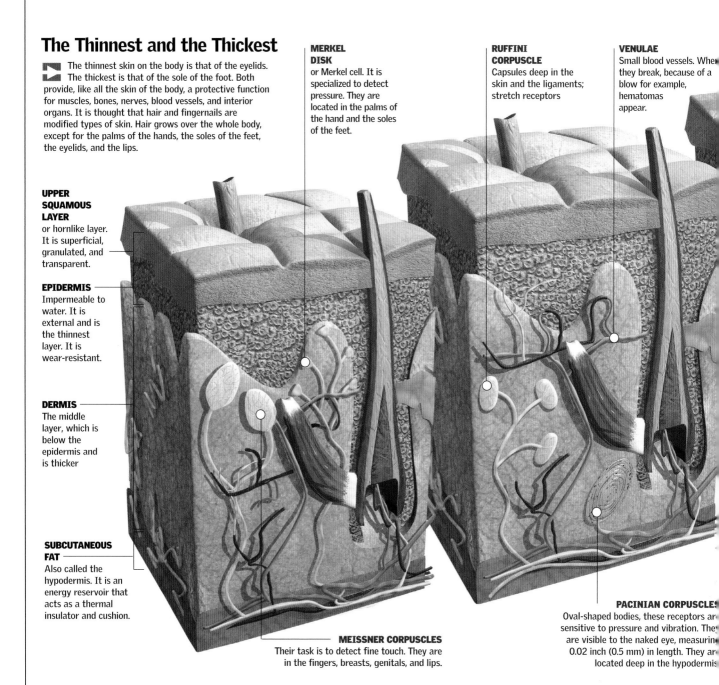

MEISSNER CORPUSCLES
Their task is to detect fine touch. They are in the fingers, breasts, genitals, and lips.

PACINIAN CORPUSCLES
Oval-shaped bodies, these receptors are sensitive to pressure and vibration. They are visible to the naked eye, measuring 0.02 inch (0.5 mm) in length. They are located deep in the hypodermis.

Skin

A MAN'S SKIN PRODUCES A
GREATER QUANTITY OF
SEBUM, OR OILY SECRETION,
THAN THAT OF A WOMAN.
THEREFORE, A MAN'S SKIN
IS TOUGHER AND GREASIER
THAN A WOMAN'S.

**SUDORIFEROUS
CONDUIT**
Sweat, a liquid
secreted by the
sudoriferous gland
and composed of
water, salts, and
toxins, passes
through this conduit.

HAIR SHAFT
The part of
the hair bulb
that extends
above the skin

**BASAL CELL
LAYER**
The deepest layer
of the epidermis

SUDORIFEROUS GLANDS
regulate the temperature of the body.
The eccrine glands are tubular and
over the entire surface of the body.
The apocrine glands are specialized;
they are located only in the armpits
and the genital area. They are large
and do not empty directly onto the
skin but into the pilous follicle.

**HAIR
FOLLICLE**
The sheath
that covers
a hair

**SEBACEOUS
GLAND**
A holocrine gland
near the surface of
the skin, it secretes
an oily substance
that coats the skin
and keeps it soft
and flexible.

BULBUS PILI (HAIR BULB)
The lower extremity of the hair. It is
thick and surrounds the nerve papilla.

Responding to Temperature

When the skin perceives the sensation of cold, the blood vessels and the muscles contract. The purpose of this is to prevent the escape of heat; as a consequence, the hairs stand on end, resulting in what is commonly called goose bumps. The opposite happens in response to heat: the blood vessels dilate because the skin has received instructions from the brain to dissipate heat, and the vessels emit heat as if they were radiators. The sudoriferous glands exude sweat onto the surface of the skin. The evaporation of sweat removes heat from the skin.

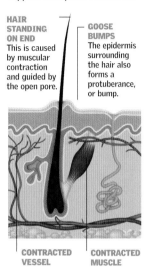

**HAIR
STANDING
ON END**
This is caused
by muscular
contraction
and guided by
the open pore.

**GOOSE
BUMPS**
The epidermis
surrounding
the hair also
forms a
protuberance,
or bump.

**CONTRACTED
VESSEL**

**CONTRACTED
MUSCLE**

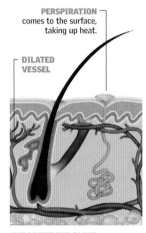

PERSPIRATION
comes to the surface,
taking up heat.

**DILATED
VESSEL**

SUDORIFEROUS GLAND
secretes sweat, which rises to the
surface of the epidermis.

A COLD
As with fear, cold puts a
person's hair on end—literally!
The contraction of both the
blood vessels and the muscles
causes the hair on the skin to
stand on end.

B HEAT
causes the secretion of sweat,
which increases as the
temperature rises. Cooling is
caused by the evaporation of the
sweat, which carries heat away
from the body.

Nails

They are hard and hornlike. Their principal component is keratin, a protein that is also present in the skin and the hair. Their function is to cover and protect the ends of the fingers and toes. Their cells arise from the proliferative matrix and advance longitudinally. Once outside the body, they die. That is why there is no pain when you cut them.

A SHIELD FOR THE FINGERS AND TOES

The fingernail can be seen with
the unaided eye, but the
protective structure of the fingers
and toes also includes their matrix
and bone structure.

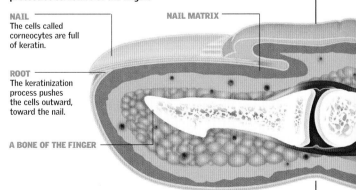

NAIL
The cells called
corneocytes are full
of keratin.

ROOT
The keratinization
process pushes
the cells outward,
toward the nail.

A BONE OF THE FINGER

NAIL MATRIX

Anatomy of the Eye

A lmost all the information that comes from the world into the brain depends on vision. The eye, one of the most complex organs of the body, allows us to judge the size and texture of an object even before we touch it or to know how far away it is. More than 100 million cells are activated instantaneously in the presence of light, converting the image perceived into nerve impulses that are transmitted to the brain. For this reason 70 percent of all the body's sensory receptors are concentrated in the eyes. It is vital that the brain receive information in a correct form: otherwise, things would appear to be distorted. ●

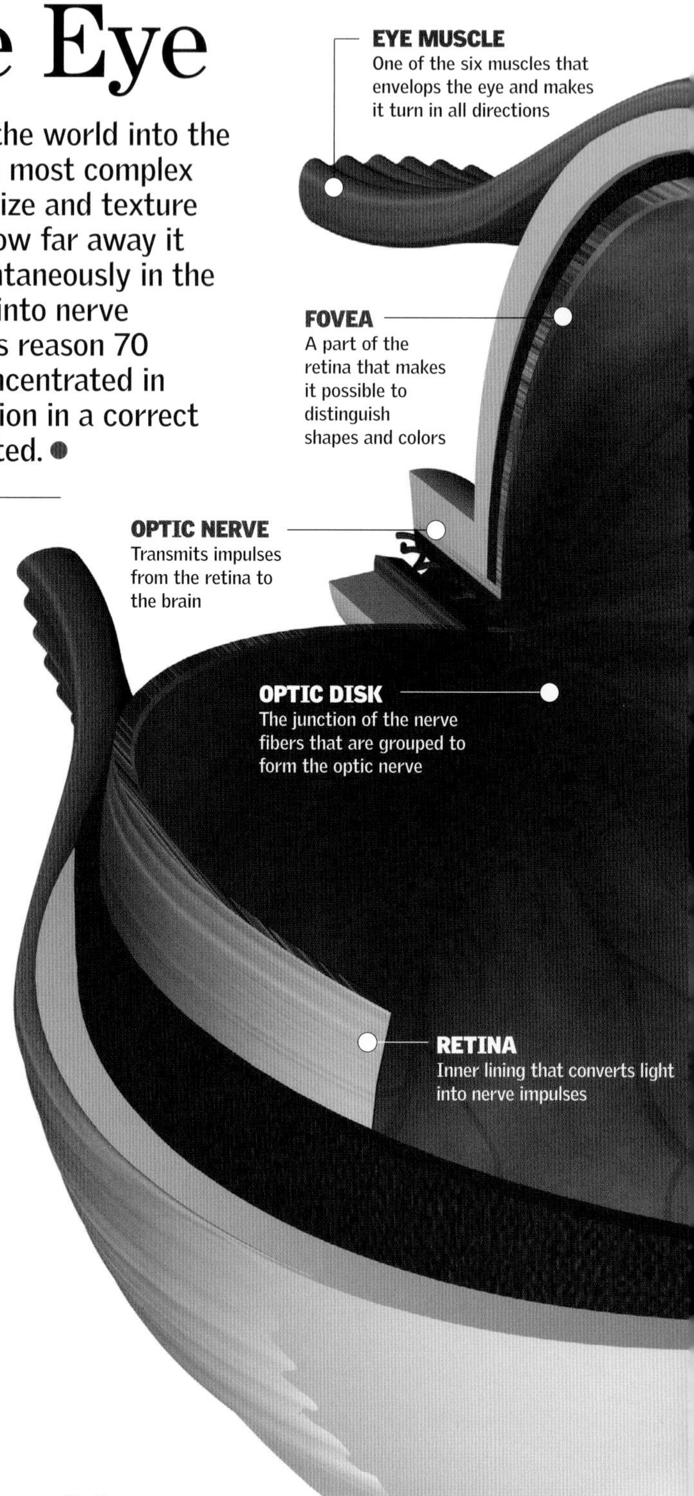

EYE MUSCLE
One of the six muscles that envelops the eye and makes it turn in all directions

FOVEA
A part of the retina that makes it possible to distinguish shapes and colors

OPTIC NERVE
Transmits impulses from the retina to the brain

OPTIC DISK
The junction of the nerve fibers that are grouped to form the optic nerve

RETINA
Inner lining that converts light into nerve impulses

How Does the Eye See?

An object reflects light in all directions. The light is partially focused by the cornea, which refracts the entering rays. The lens focuses the rays of light, changing its shape to give the light the focus it needs. The rays cross the inside of the eye. The light arrives at the retina, and the rays perceived produce an inverted image of the object. The retina sends this information to the brain, which processes it and constructs a correct image of the object. Thanks to the fovea the eye can perceive details such as the shape and color of objects.

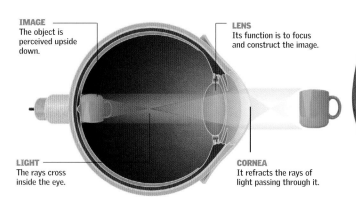

IMAGE
The object is perceived upside down.

LENS
Its function is to focus and construct the image.

LIGHT
The rays cross inside the eye.

CORNEA
It refracts the rays of light passing through it.

Seeing in Three Dimensions

When the eyes look ahead, the field of vision is binocular because both eyes see at the same time, each one from a different perspective. The images are superimposed at an angle of approximately 120°. This allows stereoscopic vision (two images of the same object from different angles, without deformation). The brain perceives the image in three dimensions.

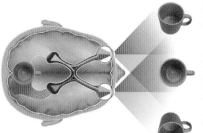

IMAGE 1
The left eye perceives an object at an angle of 45°.

IMAGE 2
The images from both eyes come together, and the brain reflects the object at a right angle.

IMAGE 3
The perception of the right eye completes the binocular arc of 120°.

Iris

A colored membranous disk, with a pupil in the center. It has two types of muscular fibers: circular and radial. In response to bright light the circular fibers contract and the radial fibers relax: the pupil diminishes in size to reduce the amount of light that enters. When there is less light, the circular muscles relax, and the radial ones contract. The pupil then dilates so that more light will enter to facilitate vision.

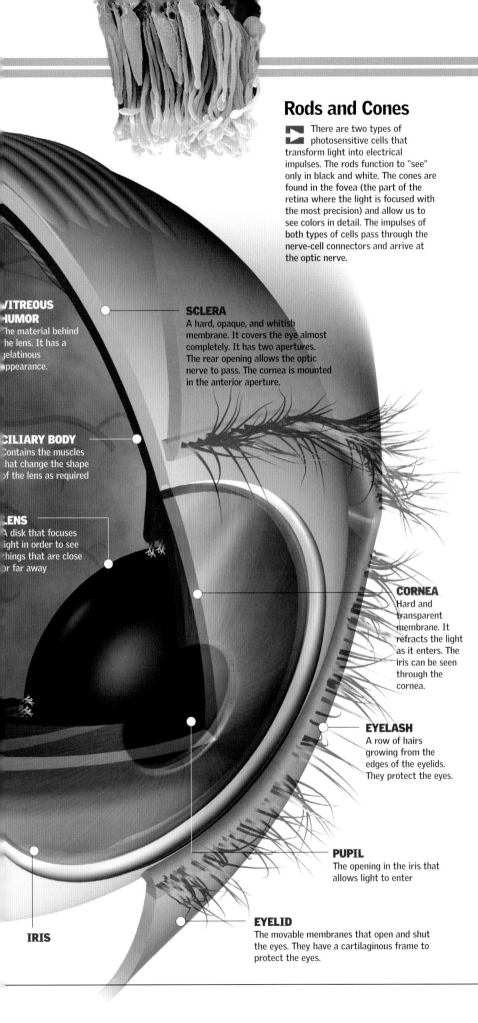

Rods and Cones

There are two types of photosensitive cells that transform light into electrical impulses. The rods function to "see" only in black and white. The cones are found in the fovea (the part of the retina where the light is focused with the most precision) and allow us to see colors in detail. The impulses of both types of cells pass through the nerve-cell connectors and arrive at the optic nerve.

VITREOUS HUMOR
The material behind the lens. It has a gelatinous appearance.

CILIARY BODY
Contains the muscles that change the shape of the lens as required

LENS
A disk that focuses light in order to see things that are close or far away

IRIS

SCLERA
A hard, opaque, and whitish membrane. It covers the eye almost completely. It has two apertures. The rear opening allows the optic nerve to pass. The cornea is mounted in the anterior aperture.

CORNEA
Hard and transparent membrane. It refracts the light as it enters. The iris can be seen through the cornea.

EYELASH
A row of hairs growing from the edges of the eyelids. They protect the eyes.

PUPIL
The opening in the iris that allows light to enter

EYELID
The movable membranes that open and shut the eyes. They have a cartilaginous frame to protect the eyes.

VISION PROBLEMS

The most common problems involve seeing things out of focus. These are hypermetropia and myopia. Both can be corrected by the use of lenses. A hereditary condition called color blindness, or Daltonism, is less frequent.

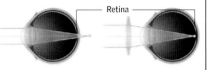

Retina

A **HYPEROPIA (FARSIGHTEDNESS)**
This condition makes it difficult to see objects that are close to us. It happens when the image is focused behind the retina. It can be corrected by convex (converging) lenses, which make the rays of light strike the retina properly.

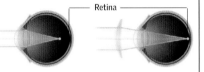

Retina

B **MYOPIA (NEARSIGHTEDNESS)**
Here the image is formed in front of the retina. This usually occurs when the ocular sphere is longer than normal. The myopic person has difficulty seeing distant objects. Myopia is corrected with concave (diverging) lenses or by an operation using a laser.

C **COLOR BLINDNESS**
Persons who are color blind have problems distinguishing between certain colors. It is a hereditary illness caused by the absence of the types of cone cells that are sensitive to yellow, green, or blue.

Protection

THE EYELIDS PROTECT THE EYES FROM BRIGHT LIGHT AND DUST. THE EYELASHES REDUCE EXCESS LIGHT. THE EYEBROWS KEEP SWEAT OUT OF THE EYES. THE NASOLACHRYMAL DUCT TAKES THE TEARS FROM THE NASAL CAVITY TO THE LACHRYMAL DUCTS—THE OPENINGS AT THE EXTREMITIES OF THE EYES—WHERE THEY ARE SECRETED.

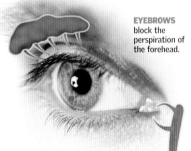

EYEBROWS
block the perspiration of the forehead.

EYELASH
They protect against excess light.

LACHRYMAL GLAND
There is one at the inner extremity of each eye.

Mechanics of Hearing

The ear is the sense responsible for hearing and maintaining equilibrium. When the ear perceives sounds, it registers its characteristics—volume, tone, and timbre—as well as the direction from which it comes. A group of nerve terminals receives information about the body's motion and transmits this to the brain in order to maintain dynamic and static equilibrium. The ear is important for communication by means of speech or other means, such as music. The ear is capable of distinguishing a great range of volumes, from the buzzing of a mosquito to the roar of an airplane. The ear contains the smallest bones of the body. ●

Frequencies

The frequency of a sound is the speed at which the sound makes the air vibrate. It is measured in units called hertz (Hz): one hertz corresponds to one vibration per second. High frequencies correspond to high sounds, and low frequencies to low sounds. The human ear can hear sounds between 20 and 20,000 vibrations per second.

FREQUENCIES AUDIBLE TO HUMANS AND ANIMALS

SUBJECT	MINIMUM	MAXIMUM
Person 10 years old	20 Hz	20,000 Hz
Person 60 years old	20 Hz	12,000 Hz
Dog	60 Hz	45,000 Hz
Frog	100 Hz	3,000 Hz
Bat	1,000 Hz	120,000 Hz
Cat	60 Hz	65,000 Hz

Organ of Corti

Contains ciliary cells that collect vibrations and transform mechanical energy into energy of the nervous system. Next the impulses arrive at the brain via the cochlear nerve. The nerve cells do not have a regenerative capacity, so if they are lost hearing will be lost along with them.

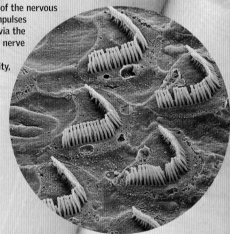

THE PROCESSING OF SOUND

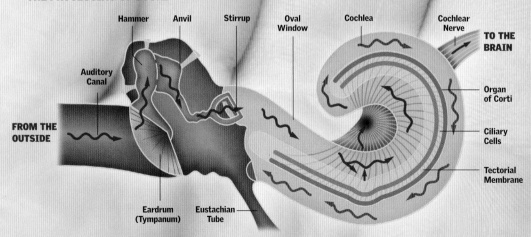

Hammer · Anvil · Stirrup · Oval Window · Cochlea · Cochlear Nerve · TO THE BRAIN

Auditory Canal

Organ of Corti

Ciliary Cells

FROM THE OUTSIDE

Tectorial Membrane

Eardrum (Tympanum) · Eustachian Tube

1 ENTRANCE
The sound wave is captured by the ear and enters via the auditory canal.

2 VIBRATION
The tympanum registers the intensity of the wave.

3 TRANSMISSION
The vibration of the eardrum is transmitted to the hammer, from the hammer to the anvil, from the anvil to the stirrup, from the stirrup to the oval window, from there to the cochlea, and from there to the cochlear nerve, whose electrical impulses are transmitted to the brain.

Equilibrium

Dynamic and static equilibrium are maintained by the inner ear. Above the cochlea there are three semicircular canals, which are spiral-shaped conduits. Inside the canals are a gelatinous membrane and thousands of cilia, or hairlike structures, traversed by a cranial nerve that connects them to the brain. When the head moves, this gelatinous membrane is displaced, and the tiny cilia send the brain information about the velocity and the direction of this displacement. On that basis the body can move as required to maintain equilibrium. Excessive motion produces seasickness, because the cilia continue to move even when the motion stops.

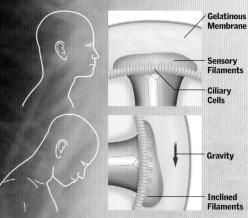

Gelatinous Membrane

Sensory Filaments

Ciliary Cells

Gravity

Inclined Filaments

Fluid

Dome

Sensory Filaments

Sense of Pressure

Displaced Dome

Inclined Filaments

LINEAR MOTION
The displacement of the gelatinous membrane, caused by a difference in height, changes the structure of the auditory cilia.

ROTATIONAL MOTION
The gelatinous membrane takes on the shape of a dome so that lateral motion will also disturb its equilibrium.

EXTERNAL EAR

AURICULAR PAVILION
or pavilion of the ear. The only visible part of the ear. It consists of cartilage and skin. It captures the sound vibrations and redirects them into the ear, preventing echo.

EXTERNAL AUDITORY CANAL
It is on average 1 inch (2.5 cm) long.

EARDRUM
It vibrates, and its vibrations are perceived by the three bones of the inner ear (hammer, anvil, and stirrup).

LIGAMENT
Maintains the hammer in its position.

HAMMER
Transmits the eardrum's vibrations. It is 0.3 inch (8 mm) long.

ANVIL
Receives the hammer's vibrations

STIRRUP
Transmits vibrations to the oval window. It is 0.15 inch (4 mm) long.

MIDDLE EAR

VESTIBULAR APPARATUS

EUSTACHIAN TUBE
Connects the middle ear with the back of the nose and the pharynx. It controls the air pressure in the ear, at times through yawning.

VESTIBULE
Oval window or labyrinth. Encased in the temporal bone, one conduit goes to the cochlea (for hearing), and two go to the semicircular canals (for equilibrium).

INNER EAR

VESTIBULAR NERVE

COCHLEAR NERVE
Brings the nerve impulses of the inner ear to the brain

COCHLEA
A tubular, spiral structure filled with fluid that receives vibrations, which are then transmitted to the brain by the organ of Corti. These vibrations produce waves in the fluid, which stimulate the cilia of the organ of Corti. The cochlea allows differences in volume to be identified.

Speech and Nonverbal Language

S peaking is the verbal expression of a language and includes articulation, which is the manner in which words are formed. However, one can make oneself understood by means other than the spoken word, such as with signs, facial expressions, or gestures. These are examples of what is called nonverbal communication, whereby even silence can be expressive. ●

Language and Speech

➤ Linguists explain that the organs of speech necessary to express language in sounds, which constitute the fundamental elements of speech, are just as independent of language as a telegraph apparatus is of the Morse code it transmits. Linguists also compare language (the verbal system of communication that is almost always written) with a symphony whose score exists independently of the musicians who play it.
The vocal cords behave like instruments. They are folds of muscle that open and close to produce sounds. When they are not producing vocal sounds, normal breathing occurs. Under the control of the brain, the vocal cords produce sounds that are modified by the lips and the tongue to create speech.

NASAL CAVITY
Adds resonance to speech

ORAL CAVITY
Acts like a resonance chamber

TONGUE
By changing its shape and position, the tongue varies the sounds produced.

ESOPHAGUS
In its respiratory function it brings in air, which is pushed by the diaphragm.

LIPS
modify sounds by changing their shape

LARYNX
Contains the vocal cords

TRACHEA
Influences speech because the air passes through it

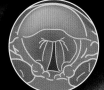

A **Passage of Air**
The vocal cords relax and open to allow air to pass to and from the lungs. No sound is produced because the vocal cords do not vibrate, which is the basis for sound.

B **Sound Is Produced.**
The vocal cords stretch horizontally above the larynx. They tighten when air flows past them. Sound is the vibration of the vocal cords.

Language of Gesture

The expressivity of the human face is the result of more than 30 muscles that tense small areas of the skin when they contract. Most of them operate in pairs. Their use is reflexive in most cases, as in the gestures, facial expressions, and grimaces that often accompany the spoken word and are silent expressions in certain situations. In other cases, however, such as the art of acting, their use and mastery can be studied and practiced. The usual example of this is the art of mimes, who can stage complete dramas that are transmitted very effectively with no recourse to the spoken word or use of the voice.

Broca
Controls the articulation of speech.

Visual
Receives and analyzes the nerve impulses from the eye.

Wernicke
comprehension language.

FACIAL EXPRESSIONS
The muscles of the face also serve to communicate feelings.

FROWNING
Action of the corrugator muscles on the eyebrows

SURPRISE
The muscles of the forehead are contracted.

SMILE
Action of the smile muscles and the zygomaticus major

Control Centers

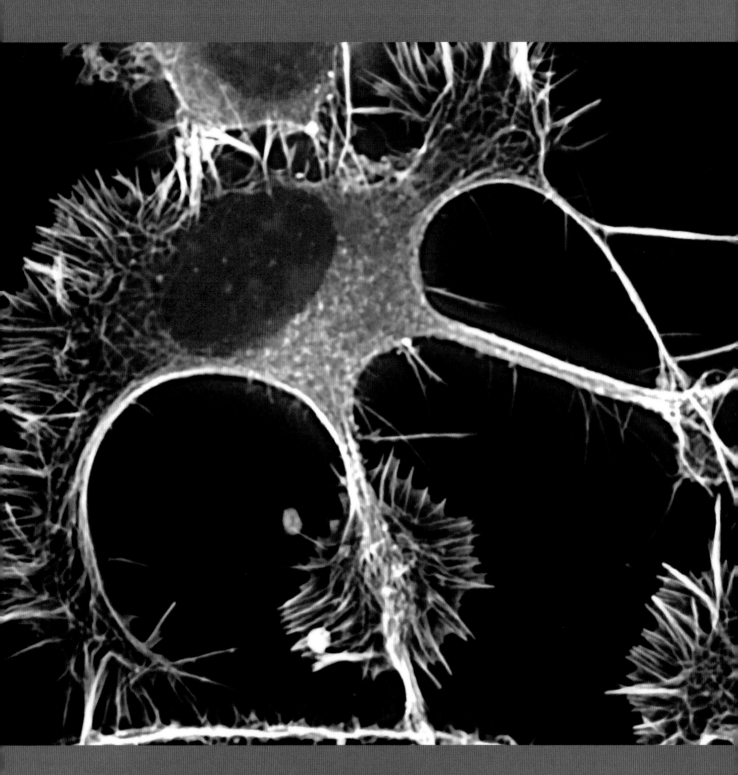

B rain tissue consists of thousands of millions of neurons that continually send each other signals through connections called synapses.

Thanks to this network the brain can remember, calculate, decide, think, dream, create, and express emotions. We invite you to understand the secrets about how these activities of the brain

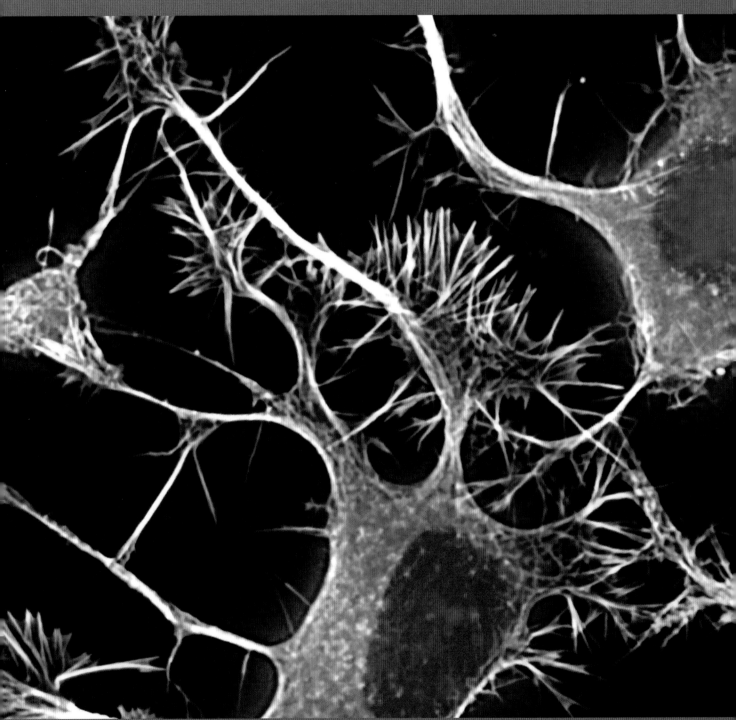

NERVE CELLS
Microscope
photograph of a
group of neurons

NERVOUS SYSTEM 82-83

NEURONS 84-85

THE BRAIN 86-87

THE PERIPHERAL NERVES 88-89

DREAM AND MEMORY 90-91

are accomplished. What determines the formation of synapses and neuronal networks? Where are intelligence and memory located? Is it possible to stimulate brain cells? What happens during a dream? What are nerves, and how are they formed? What functions are carried out by each region of the brain? You will find all this and much more in this chapter, including incredible images. ●

Nervous System

The body's most complex system, many of whose characteristics and potentialities are still unknown. Together with the endocrine system, the brain has the job of controlling the organism. Its specific functions are rapid and intellectual activities, such as memory, emotions, and will. The brain is divided into three portions: the central (the brain and the spinal cord), the peripheral (nerves of the spinal cord and cranium), and the vegetative (or autonomic function). ●

The Great Coordinator

The nervous system acts as the great coordinator of the functions of all the parts and organs of the body. In simpler organisms, such as unicellular organisms, the same cell receives sensations and responds to them without requiring intermediation or specialized coordination. However, in more complex organisms such as the human body, the cells of the different parts of the body are differentiated, as are the functions of the organs that these cells make up. Thus there are receptor cells, which receive stimuli (such as the cells of the organs linked to the eye or the senses). There are also effector cells (such as those of the muscles or the glands), which are involved in the organism's responses. The nervous system links these functions together through its three principal parts: the brain, the spinal cord, and the nerves in general. The nerves consist of numerous axons and dendrites, enveloped by a sheath of conjunctive tissue. These groups of neurons are called ganglia when they are outside the brain and the spinal cord, and they are called nuclei when they are inside.

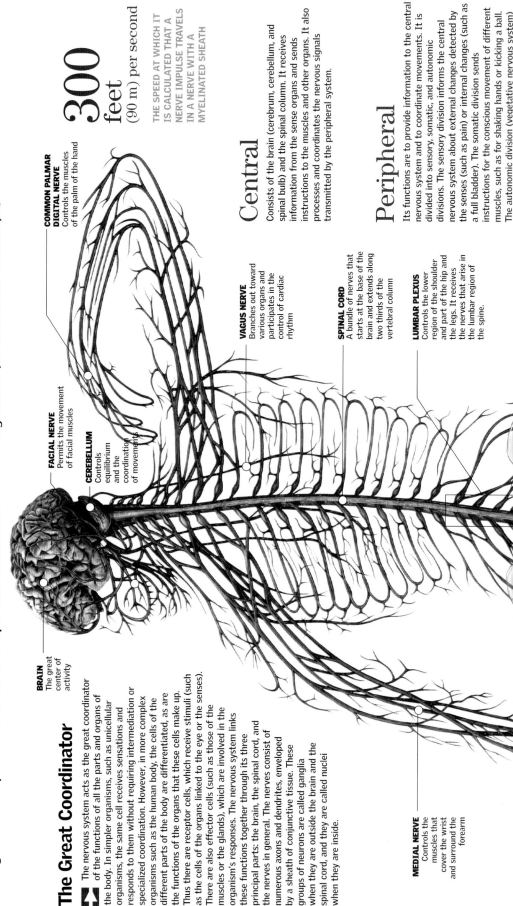

BRAIN
The great center of activity

FACIAL NERVE
Permits the movement of facial muscles

CEREBELLUM
Controls equilibrium and the coordination of movements

MEDIAL NERVE
Controls the muscles that cover the wrist and surround the forearm

COMMON PALMAR DIGITAL NERVE
Controls the muscles of the palm of the hand

VAGUS NERVE
Branches out toward various organs and participates in the control of cardiac rhythm

SPINAL CORD
A bundle of nerves that starts at the base of the brain and extends along two thirds of the vertebral column

LUMBAR PLEXUS
Controls the lower region of the shoulder and part of the hip and the legs. It receives the nerves that arise in the lumbar region of the spine.

300 feet
(90 m) per second

THE SPEED AT WHICH IT IS CALCULATED THAT A NERVE IMPULSE TRAVELS IN A NERVE WITH A MYELINATED SHEATH

Central

Consists of the brain (cerebrum, cerebellum, and spinal bulb) and the spinal column. It receives information from the sense organs and sends instructions to the muscles and other organs. It also processes and coordinates the nervous signals transmitted by the peripheral system.

Peripheral

Its functions are to provide information to the central nervous system and to coordinate movements. It is divided into sensory, somatic, and autonomic divisions. The sensory division informs the central nervous system about external changes detected by the senses (such as pain) or internal changes (such as a full bladder). The somatic division sends instructions for the conscious movement of different muscles, such as for shaking hands or kicking a ball. The autonomic division (vegetative nervous system) automatically controls the functioning of the internal

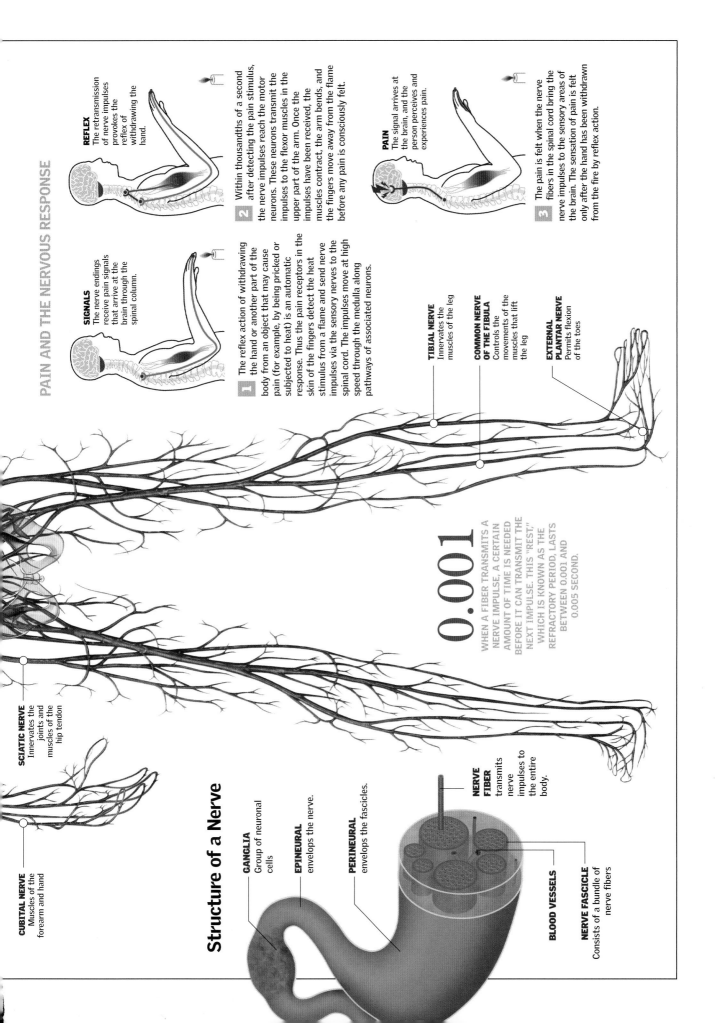

SIGNALS
The nerve endings receive pain signals that arrive at the brain through the spinal column.

REFLEX
The retransmission of nerve impulses provokes the reflex of withdrawing the hand.

1 The reflex action of withdrawing the hand or another part of the body from an object that may cause pain (for example, by being pricked or subjected to heat) is an automatic response. Thus the pain receptors in the skin of the fingers detect the heat stimulus from a flame and send nerve impulses via the sensory nerves to the spinal cord. The impulses move at high speed through the medulla along pathways of associated neurons.

2 Within thousandths of a second after detecting the pain stimulus, the nerve impulses reach the motor neurons. These neurons transmit the impulses to the flexor muscles in the upper part of the arm. Once the impulses have been received, the muscles contract, the arm bends, and the fingers move away from the flame before any pain is consciously felt.

PAIN
The signal arrives at the brain, and the person perceives and experiences pain.

3 The pain is felt when the nerve fibers in the spinal cord bring the nerve impulses to the sensory areas of the brain. The sensation of pain is felt only after the hand has been withdrawn from the fire by reflex action.

Structure of a Nerve

CUBITAL NERVE
Muscles of the forearm and hand

SCIATIC NERVE
Innervates the joints and muscles of the hip tendon

TIBIAL NERVE
Innervates the muscles of the leg

COMMON NERVE OF THE FIBULA
Controls the movements of the muscles that lift the leg

EXTERNAL PLANTAR NERVE
Permits flexion of the toes

GANGLIA
Group of neuronal cells

EPINEURAL
envelops the nerve.

PERINEURAL
envelops the fascicles.

NERVE FIBER
transmits nerve impulses to the entire body.

BLOOD VESSELS

NERVE FASCICLE
Consists of a bundle of nerve fibers

0.001
WHEN A FIBER TRANSMITS A NERVE IMPULSE, A CERTAIN AMOUNT OF TIME IS NEEDED BEFORE IT CAN TRANSMIT THE NEXT IMPULSE. THIS "REST," WHICH IS KNOWN AS THE REFRACTORY PERIOD, LASTS BETWEEN 0.001 AND 0.005 SECOND.

Neurons

Neurons are cells that make up the nervous system. Their function is to transmit impulses in the form of electrical signals carrying information to the brain and from there to the periphery. The neurons provide the basis for the system's activities and form a highly complex communication network. They are surrounded and protected by other nerve cells that are not excitable, called glial cells, which constitute more than half of all an organism's nerve cells. ●

Plasticity

Each neuron is essentially made up of a body, an axon, and many dendrites. The communication that is established among neurons resembles a conversation, or a continuous ongoing exchange of information. Until recently it was thought that neurons, unlike other tissue, could not be regenerated once lost. Today not only is it known that this is not so, but it is also known that the capabilities of the brain and the nervous system are more a function of the circuits and connections that are established among the neurons than of the number of neurons per se. These connections are activated, deactivated, and modified by very diverse factors (such as learning, food, habits, exercise, the effects of drugs and accidents). Some neurons can regenerate if they have been damaged.

SYNAPTIC NODE
The terminal point of the axon branch, it contains chemicals that transmit nerve impulses.

MYELIN SHEATH
A fatty layer that insulates the axons of some neurons in order to accelerate nerve impulse transmission. In the peripheral nervous system, this sheath consists of Schwann cells.

RANVIER'S NODE
An opening in the myelin sheath that aids in the transmission of nerve impulse

MITOCHONDRIA
provide energy to the cell.

AXON
Nerve fiber that transmits impulses

NUCLEUS
Contains the neuron's genetic material

SCHWANN CELL
A glial cell that surrounds an axon

Generates the vital processes of the neuron cell

500 million

IS THE NUMBER OF SYNAPSES (CONNECTIONS AMONG NEURONS) FORMED IN 0.06 CUBIC INCH (1 CU MM) OF A BRAIN'S NERVE TISSUE. OVERALL, THE BRAIN HAS 1 QUADRILLION SYNAPSES.

DENDRITE
Protuberance that captures signals from other neurons. A neuron can have about 200 dendrites; the number of dendrites varies from cell to cell.

100 billion

THE NUMBER OF INTERCONNECTED NEURONS IN A HUMAN BEING

Transmission and Synapses

The synapse is the point of communication between neurons. It comprises a synaptic cleft, a synaptic knob, and a target to which the nerve signal is directed. In order for a neuron to be activated, there must be a stimulus that converts the electrical charge inside the membrane of the cell from negative to positive. The nerve impulse travels via the axon toward the synaptic knob and brings about the release of chemical substances called neurotransmitters. These in turn can elicit a response from the target to which the stimulus is directed.

Neuromuscular Union

This is a special kind of synapse between the neurons and the skeletal muscle fibers that causes voluntary contraction of the muscles.

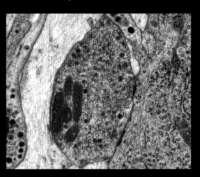

The axon of a neuron links itself with a muscle fiber. At the point of contact a chemical synapse is produced between the neuron and an effector, a muscle with electrically excitable tissue, and movement results.

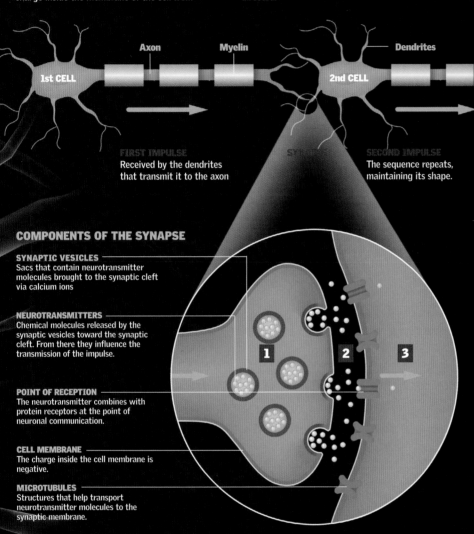

Axon **Myelin** **Dendrites**

1st CELL **2nd CELL**

FIRST IMPULSE
Received by the dendrites that transmit it to the axon

SYNAPSE

SECOND IMPULSE
The sequence repeats, maintaining its shape.

COMPONENTS OF THE SYNAPSE

SYNAPTIC VESICLES
Sacs that contain neurotransmitter molecules brought to the synaptic cleft via calcium ions

NEUROTRANSMITTERS
Chemical molecules released by the synaptic vesicles toward the synaptic cleft. From there they influence the transmission of the impulse.

POINT OF RECEPTION
The neurotransmitter combines with protein receptors at the point of neuronal communication.

CELL MEMBRANE
The charge inside the cell membrane is negative.

MICROTUBULES
Structures that help transport neurotransmitter molecules to the synaptic membrane.

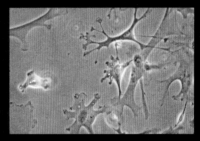

ASTROCYTES are cells located in cerebral tissue, where they exceed neurons in number. Astrocytes have some delicate protuberances that are linked to the blood vessels and that regulate the flow of nutrients and waste between neurons and blood.

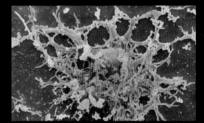

TRANSMISSION OF NERVE IMPULSES

1 Without Information
When the neuron is at rest, the sodium ions inside it are uniformly distributed so that the electrical charge inside the cell membrane is permanently negative.

2 The Impulse Arrives
The arrival of the neurotransmissions at the dendrites causes a reversal of the charge, which becomes positive in this area, giving it a tendency to move in the direction of the negatively charged part of the cell.

3 Transmission of Information
The positive charge travels toward the negatively charged axon until it reaches the synapse and thus the other cell. The areas it has left return to their stable (negative) state.

OLIGODENDROCYTES are the cells that form the myelin sheath around the nerve fibers of the brain and the spinal column. Their function is similar to that of Schwann cells in the peripheral nervous system

TYPES OF NEURONS ACCORDING TO THEIR COMPLEXITY

UNIPOLAR. Two branches of the same axon extend from one cell body.

BIPOLAR. Two separate axons extend from each end of a cell body.

MULTIPOLAR. One axon and a number of dendrites extend from a cell body.

The Brain

The brain is the body's control center. Underneath its folds more than 100 billion neurons organize and examine incoming information and act as a guide for the organism. In spite of amounting to only 2 percent of the total weight of a human body, the brain alone uses one fifth of the oxygen inhaled. It is one of the most fragile parts of the body and, therefore, one of the most protected. Along with the spinal cord, the brain forms the central nervous system, which gives instructions to the peripheral nervous system.

3 pounds (1.4 kg)

AVERAGE WEIGHT OF AN ADULT BRAIN. AT BIRTH THE BRAIN WEIGHS BETWEEN 12 AND 14 OUNCES (350 AND 400 G).

MENINGES
Protective membranes covering the brain

PIAMATER

DURA MATER

CRANIAL BONE

CEPHALO-SPINAL LIQUID

ARACHNOIDS

BRAIN

BLOOD VESSEL

Parietal Lobe
In Latin parietal means "wall." Located on the sides, this area receives sensory information and influences spatial orientation.

Occipital Lobe
Detects and interprets visual images

Temporal Lobe
Where sound and its pitch and volume are recognized. The temporal lobe plays an important role in the storage of memories.

THALAMUS
Retransmits nerve signals to the cerebral cortex

HYPOTHALAMUS
Controls the endocrine system (produces hormones)

Cerebellum
Associated with controlling the body's equilibrium

Meninges

There are three membranes, called meninges, that cover the brain. The outermost one covers the inside of the cranium, and it contains veins and arteries that feed blood to the cranial bones. It is called dura mater. The middle membrane is known as the arachnoid and consists of netlike elastic connective tissue. The piamater, the thinnest of the three, is the closest to the surface of the cerebral cortex. Its functions are primarily protective.

On one hand it acts as a filter to prevent the entry of harmful substances and microorganisms into the nervous system. On the other hand, as the covering of the most important organ of the body, it acts like an elastic helmet (remember that death takes place when the brain ceases to function). The cephalo-spinal liquid, a transparent fluid that acts like a shock absorber, circulates within the meninges.

CEREBRAL CORTEX
Gray matter. It is between 0.08 and 0.24 inch (2 and 6 mm) thick. The white matter is underneath.

Frontal Lobe

Contains neurons that govern the production of speech, the elaboration of thought and emotion, and the performance of complex movements

CALLUS BODY
A bundle of nerve fibers that connect the two cerebral hemispheres

MAP OF THE BRAIN

PRIMARY SENSORY CORTEX
Receives signals from the sensory receptors in the skin

SENSORY ASSOCIATION CORTEX
Areas of the cortex that do not process sensory or motor information

VISUAL ASSOCIATION CORTEX
Forms images by association and analysis of information

PRIMARY VISUAL CORTEX
Receives sensory information sent by the eyes

MOTOR CORTEX
Sends instructions to the muscles telling them to contract

WERNICKE'S AREA
Linguistic area for auditory decoding

PRE-MOTOR CORTEX
Coordinates complex movements of the muscle motor area

PRE-FRONTAL CORTEX
Promotes the development of reasoning and planning (area of association and analysis of information)

BROCA'S AREA
Speech production. It is a motor area that commands the phonation muscles.

PRIMARY AUDITORY CORTEX
A sensory area. It receives information from the sensory receptors of the eyes.

ASSOCIATIVE AUDITORY CORTEX
Area for association and analysis of sounds

Spinal Medulla

The spinal medulla is the spinal cord, which goes from the cephalic trunk to the lumbar region. Together with the brain it forms the central nervous system. It can reach a length of 18 inches (45 cm). It is composed of gray and white matter. The gray matter is located in its core, in tissue consisting essentially of neurons.

Surrounding the gray matter is white matter that contains the nerve fibers that transmit signals to and from the brain. The spinal nerves extend outward from the medulla to the body and its extremities. Paralysis in one or more parts of the body can result if the spinal cord is damaged.

Gray and White Matter

The so-called gray matter, located in the cerebral cortex and in the spinal column, consists of groups of neuronal cells. White matter, on the other hand, consists primarily of myelin-sheathed axons or nerves that extend from the neuron cell bodies. The fatty layers of myelin allow for an increase in the transmission speed of nerve impulses.

GRAY MATTER

WHITE MATTER

MENINGES

SENSORY ROOT OF THE NERVE

ROOT OF THE MOTOR NERVE

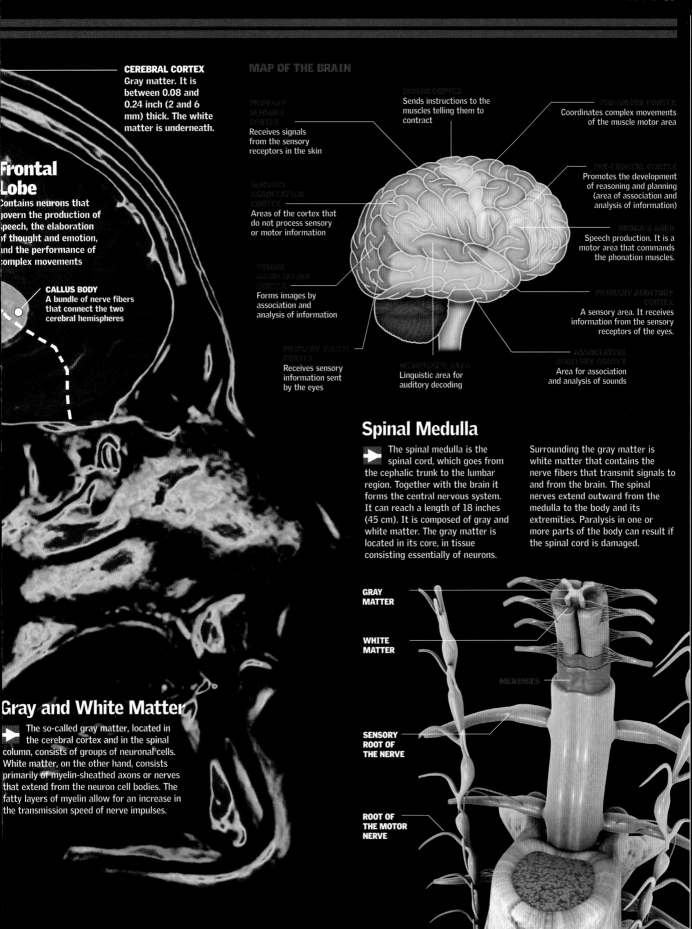

Peripheral Nerves

The peripheral nerves have the task of bringing information to and from the brain and spinal column. Depending on their location, they may be cranial or spinal nerves. The sensory fibers in the peripheral nerves receive information from the outside world, the skin, and the internal organs and transmit it to the central nervous system; the motor fibers begin to contract the skeletal muscles and transmit signals in the opposite direction from the sensors. The nerves are located deep in the body, with some exceptions, such as the cubital nerve in the elbow. ●

Spinal Nerves

There are 31 pairs of spinal nerves that begin at the spinal cord and extend through the spaces between the vertebrae. Each nerve is divided into numerous branches. These nerves control most of the body's skeletal muscles, as well as the smooth muscles and the glands. The cervical nerves serve the muscles of the chest and shoulders. The lumbar nerves serve the abdomen and part of the legs, and the sacral nerves control the rest of the legs and the feet.

THORACIC SPINAL NERVES
Twelve pairs. The anterior branch forms the intercostals.

LUMBAR SPINAL NERVES
Five pairs. The last ones form the "horse's tail."

SACRAL SPINAL NERVES
Five pairs. They are located in the lowest segment of the spinal cord.

SPINAL CERVICAL NERVES
Eight pairs. They innervate the neck.

COCCYGEAL SPINAL NERVE
The only unpaired spinal nerve, it is located in the tailbone, or coccyx.

THE THREE RESPONSES

The nerve receptors gather information that goes to the cerebral cortex and to the spinal cord. The response can be automatic, ordering dilation or contraction. Voluntary response implies a complex nerve path. Reflex responses are simpler; some of them are processed in the brain, but most of them are processed in the spinal cord.

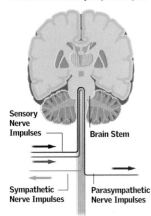

Sensory Nerve Impulses — Brain Stem

Sympathetic Nerve Impulses — Parasympathetic Nerve Impulses

A | AUTOMATIC RESPONSE
The impulses, or sympathetic (dilation) or parasympathetic (contraction) response signals, travel over separate pathways.

Cerebral Cortex

Sensory Nerve Impulse

Cerebellum

Motor Nerve Impulse — Spinal Cord

B | VOLUNTARY RESPONSE
The sensory impulses that activate voluntary responses occur in various areas of the brain. The nerve path is complex.

Sensory Nerve Impulse — Spinal Cord

Motor Nerve Impulse

C | REFLEXES
Some are processed in the brain, but most of them are processed in the spinal cord, where the impulse is processed and the reply is sent.

Cranial Nerves

The 12 pairs of cranial nerves extend fro the lower part of the brain, as can be se the main illustration. Except for the vagus ner the cranial nerves control the muscles of the in the neck region or bring nerve impulses fro sense organs, such as the eyes, to the brain. Ir case of nerve impulses that come from the ey is the pair of optical nerves that record the sensations from the retina of the eye. The olfactory nerve works the same way for the n

PAIR II
Optic nerve. Supplies the retina. Transmits signals, from the photo receptors, perceived as vision.

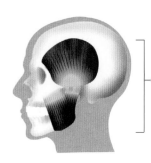

PAIR V
Trigeminal nerve. Controls the muscles involved in chewing and transmits sensory information from the eyes, the teeth, and the side of the face.

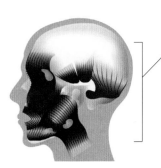

PAIR VII
Facial nerve. Controls the muscles of facial expressions and the salivary and tear glands. Transmits sensory information from the taste buds.

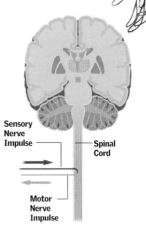

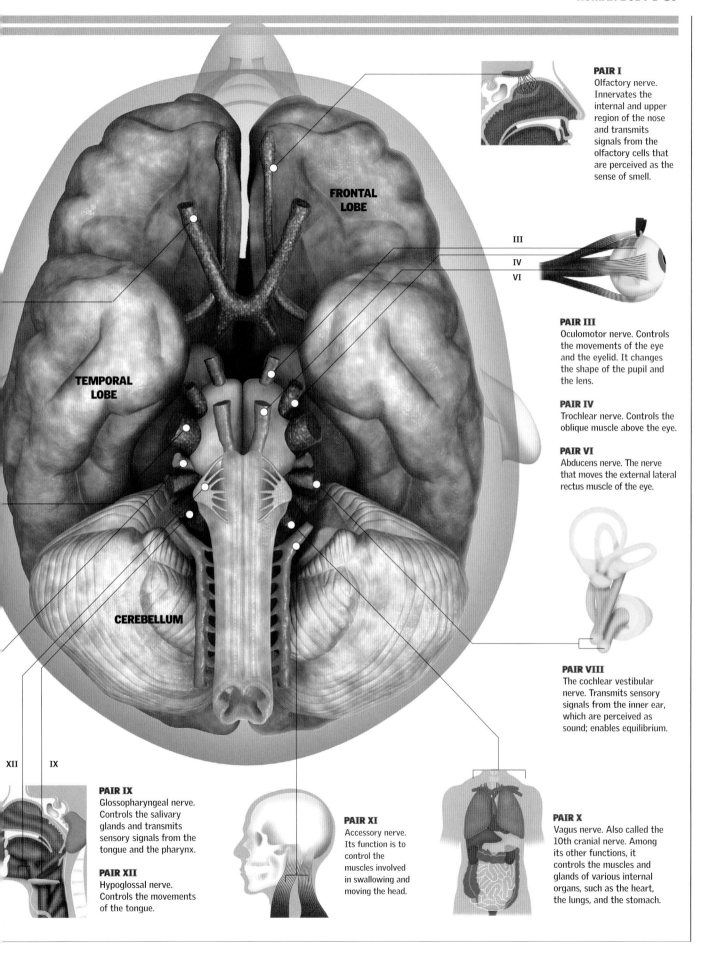

FRONTAL LOBE

TEMPORAL LOBE

CEREBELLUM

III

IV

VI

XII   IX

PAIR I
Olfactory nerve. Innervates the internal and upper region of the nose and transmits signals from the olfactory cells that are perceived as the sense of smell.

PAIR III
Oculomotor nerve. Controls the movements of the eye and the eyelid. It changes the shape of the pupil and the lens.

PAIR IV
Trochlear nerve. Controls the oblique muscle above the eye.

PAIR VI
Abducens nerve. The nerve that moves the external lateral rectus muscle of the eye.

PAIR VIII
The cochlear vestibular nerve. Transmits sensory signals from the inner ear, which are perceived as sound; enables equilibrium.

PAIR IX
Glossopharyngeal nerve. Controls the salivary glands and transmits sensory signals from the tongue and the pharynx.

PAIR XII
Hypoglossal nerve. Controls the movements of the tongue.

PAIR XI
Accessory nerve. Its function is to control the muscles involved in swallowing and moving the head.

PAIR X
Vagus nerve. Also called the 10th cranial nerve. Among its other functions, it controls the muscles and glands of various internal organs, such as the heart, the lungs, and the stomach.

Dream and Memory

To be able to process the information gathered during the day, the brain takes advantage of periodic dream states. During a dream the brain reduces its activities, and its patterns of thought are disconnected from the external world. The passage from consciousness to dreaming (and from dreaming to consciousness) is the task of neurotransmitters, chemical substances that are manufactured and released from the reticular activator system, a regulator in the cephalic talus, which lies in the brain stem. ●

CINGULAR GYRUS
Changes behavior and emotions

HIPPOCAMPUS
Stores short-term memory and converts it into long-term memory

PREFRONTAL CORTEX
Retains short-term memory

THALAMUS

OLFACTORY BULB
Sends information related to the sense of smell to the limbic system

AMYGDALA
Stores fears and phobias

TEMPORAL LOBE
Stores semantic memory

CEREBELLUM
Controls movement and equilibrium

Formation of Memory

Memory is a set of processes in which unconscious associations are capable of retaining and recording highly varied information. This information can be perceived consciously or unconsciously and ranges from ideas and concepts to sensations that were previously experienced or processed. Memory has many forms, but the two basic ones are the long-term and short-term memory.

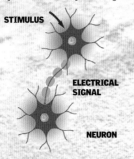

STIMULUS

ELECTRICAL SIGNAL

NEURON

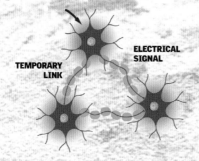

TEMPORARY LINK

ELECTRICAL SIGNAL

1 **CONNECTION.** An experience triggers a pattern (or model to be repeated), exciting two neutrons. To form long-term memory the template that was generated earlier by the short-term memory must be replicated. When a stimulus is received, the neuron reacts, sending an impulse to a neighboring neuron.

2 **LINK FORMATION.** The nerve impulses sent to the neighboring neurons generate a greater capacity for response from the cells that sent the impulses. A temporary union is formed among the cells. In the future, they will be more likely to trigger a nerve impulse together. A neuronal template is beginning to be created.

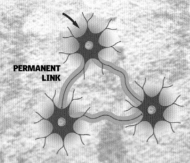

PERMANENT LINK

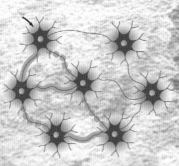

3 **DEEPER LINKS.** Every time an event is remembered, a nerve impulse is triggered. As a recollection is repeated, the neurons become more solidly connected. Then the neurons begin to send joint impulses, no matter which was excited first. The development of connections is strengthened with repetition or notable or stressful events.

4 **EXPANDING NETWORK.** With successive repetition, different groups of neurons begin to form a neuronal network that represents the long-term memory. The more complex the network, the more accessible and durable the memory will be. Each group of neuronal cells represents a different aspect through which one accesses the complete memory.

20 seconds

THE TIME AFTER WHICH SHORT-TERM MEMORY LOSES INFORMATION (SUCH AS A TELEPHONE NUMBER) THAT HAS NOT BEEN USED

Limbic System

Consists of a complex of structures that wrap around the upper part of the brain stem. These structures control emotions such as annoyance and happiness. They protect us from danger and play an important role in memory formation. For example, the amygdala produces fear when processing danger. The hippocampus permits us to store and remember short-term memories that are brought to the cortex. When the hippocampus is damaged, new memories cannot be incorporated.

REM

The acronym for Rapid Eye Movement. The eyes move, though the body is stationary.

Dream Patterns

A pattern is a model that serves as a template, or mold, to obtain the same format. During sleep the two great patterns are REM and NREM, with their four phases. REM sleep is the most enigmatic; it is thought that dreams are produced during REM. During that time the human being lives out an inner experience, generally involuntary, where the mind provides representations of sensations, images, situations, dialogues, sounds, etc.

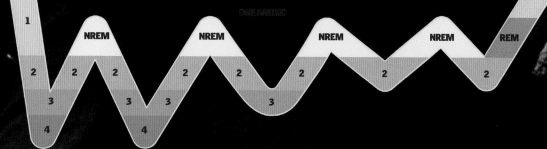

PHASE 1
Transition between waking and sleeping. The electroencephalograph (EEG), a device that measures cerebral activity, registers alpha waves. The body is relaxed, but if someone disturbs the sleeping person then he or she will wake up.

PHASE 2
Second-phase NREM. The EEG pattern is more irregular. Waking up the person is more difficult.

PHASE 3
Delta waves appear. The vital signs decrease: respiration and the heartbeat slow down, and the body temperature falls.

PHASE 4
Now the dream phase or phase of deep sleep occurs. The delta waves are dominant, and the vital signs drop to minimal levels.

PHASE REM
Rapid Eye Movement. The vital signs increase. The skeletal muscles become inhibited. Dreams enter the scene.

Glossary

Acid

Substance that, in solution, increases the concentration of hydrogen ions and combines with bases to form salts.

Adrenaline

Hormone secreted primarily by the adrenal medulla of the adrenal glands. It constricts blood vessels and is used as a medicine.

Allele

Gene variant that encodes a trait. One diploid cell contains one allele of each parent for each characteristic.

Amino Acid

Organic chemical whose molecular composition includes an amino group (derived from ammonia) and a carboxyl group (a radical that characterizes organic acids).

Antigen

Substance that causes an immune response, such as the production of antibodies, when introduced into the body.

Aorta

Largest artery in the body, originating in the left ventricle of the heart. Down to the diaphragm it is called the thoracic aorta and then the abdominal or ventral aorta to the point where it branches.

Aortic Arch

Curve in the aortic artery near its origin at the heart. The arch has the shape of a shepherd's crook.

Apparatus

Complex of organs that fulfills one function. In the physiology of the human body it is also used as a synonym for system. For example, the digestive apparatus, reproductive apparatus, or respiratory apparatus.

Artery

Blood vessel that brings blood from the heart to the entire body.

Arthroscopy

Surgical procedure used by orthopedic surgeons to inspect, diagnose, and treat problems in the joints. It consists of making a small incision and inserting an arthroscope, an instrument the size of a pencil that contains a small lens and a lighting system to magnify and illuminate the interior. The light is transmitted via fiber optics to the end of the arthroscope, and the interior of the joint can be observed via a miniature television camera.

Articulation

Joint between two bones of the body.

ATP

Adenosine triphosphate. A molecule produced primarily by mitochondria that functions as the primary energy source for the cells.

Atrium

The name for each of the two chambers of the heart that receive blood from the veins.

Basal Metabolism

Activity level of the body functions during rest or while fasting.

Bones

Rigid structures, rich in calcium, that make up the skeleton.

Carpal

The structure of the wrist, composed of eight connected bones arranged in two rows. On the side toward the arm it joins with the cubital and radial bones, and on the side toward the hand it joins with the metacarpal bones.

Cartilage

Flexible skeletal tissue consisting of isolated groups of cells within a collagenous matrix.

Celiac Artery

Artery that brings blood from the heart to the stomach and the other organs of the abdomen.

Cellular Membrane

The flexible covering of all living cells, which contains the cytoplasm. It regulates the exchange of water and gases between the cell and its exterior.

Chromatin

Complex substance in the cell nucleus composed of nucleic acid and proteins.

Cilium

Tiny hairlike protuberance on a cell with a locomotive function in a liquid medium.

Coagulation

Organic process in which the blood turns from a liquid to a solid state and whose normal purpose is to stop bleeding.

Coccyx

Bone formed by the fusion of the last vertebrae. At its base it articulates with the sacral bone. In human beings and other vertebrates that do not have a tail, it is an actual bone.

Coronal

A name given to the frontal bone, located at the anterior and superior part of the cranium. At birth the frontal bone or coronal is divided into two halves, which fuse over time. In medicine this can also refer to a suture that joins the frontal bone with the two parietal bones.

Coronary Arteries

A pair of arteries, originating in the aortic artery, that branch out and supply blood to the heart.

Cortex

The gray material present in most areas of the brain. It is the largest part of the central nervous system. The majority of the most advanced functions occur in the cortex.

Corticoids

Hormonal steroids produced by the adrenal gland cortex. Corticoids can be produced artificially. They have a therapeutic application as anti-inflammatory drugs.

Cystoscope

Apparatus used to explore the inner surface of the bladder.

Cytoplasm

A compartment of eukaryotic cells, bounded by a cellular membrane and the membranes of the cell's organelles.

Diaphragm

Respiratory muscle between the thorax and the abdomen.

Digestion

The set of processes through which the digestive system converts food into substances that can be assimilated by the organism.

Diploid

A cell with two complete sets of chromosomes. It is denoted by the symbol 2n.

Dislocation

The displacement of any bone from its normal position in a joint.

DNA

Deoxyribonucleic acid. A double helix molecule containing encoded genetic information.

Ejaculation

The action of expelling semen.

Embryo

The result of the fertilization of an ovum by a sperm cell. It can develop to become a mature organism.

Emulgent Arteries

Arteries that bring blood from the heart to the kidneys, also called renal arteries.

Endocardium

Membrane that lines the walls of the heart. It consists of two layers: an exterior, consisting of connective tissue, and an interior, of endothelial tissue.

Endometrium

Mucous membrane covering the inner walls of the uterus.

Endoplasmatic Reticulum

Network of membranes in the cell that are interconnected through the cytoplasm and whose function is the synthesis and assembly of proteins.

Endothelial

Organic tissue that lines wall-like structures within the body, such as those of the pleura or of blood vessels.

Enzyme

Protein that helps regulate the chemical processes within a cell.

Erythropoiesis

The creation of red blood cells, stimulated by the action of a protein called erythropoietin.

Follicle

Inward fold of the epidermis in the form of a sac, which usually surrounds the base of a hair.

Gene

Unit of information of a chromosome; it is a sequence of nucleotides in a DNA molecule that fulfills a specific function.

Gland

Organ that has the function of producing secretions that can be expelled through the skin or mucous membranes (salivary glands or sweat glands, for example) or into the bloodstream (the thyroid, for example).

Haploid

From the Greek *haplous*, meaning single. A haploid cell has a single set of chromosomes, unlike the diploid cells. Gametes are haploid.

Hemostatic

Substance or agent that halts hemorrhaging.

Hippocampus

Part of the brain that governs the memory.

Holocrine

Gland with an exclusively secretory function or whose secretion consists of disintegrated cells of the gland itself, such as the sebaceous glands.

Homeostasis

Complex of self-regulatory phenomena that keep the composition and the properties of the body's internal environment constant. It is said that homeostasis is reached when the body's internal environment contains the optimum concentrations of gases, nutrients, ions, and water; when its temperature is optimum; and when the volume of fluids is optimum for the life of the cells.

Hormone

The product of the glandular secretion whose function is to stimulate, inhibit, or regulate the action of other glands, systems, or organs of the body.

Innominate Bones

A pair of bones, one in each hip, which join the sacrum and the coccyx to form the pelvis. They consist of the fusion of the iliac, the ischium, and the pubic bones.

Lobes

Rounded protuberances of organs, such as the liver, the lungs, or the brain.

Lysosome

Protein that can break down the constituent substances of the walls of certain bacteria and is, hence, a potent antibacterial.

Meiosis

Type of cell division in which two successive divisions of the nucleus of a diploid cell create four haploid nuclei. As a result of this mechanism, gametes or spores are produced.

Meristem

Tissue with cells that produce other cells by cellular division.

Metabolism

Complex of chemical reactions that take place continuously within cells to synthesize complex substances from simpler substances or to degrade a substance into simpler substances. An example is the digestive process.

Metacarpal

Middle part of the skeletal structure of the hand, between the wrist (carpal bones) and the phalanges. It consists of five bones, which are the largest bones of the hand.

Metatarsal

Part of the skeletal structure of the foot, between the tarsus (posterior part of the foot) and the phalanges (toes). It consists of five bones and is usually called the sole of the foot.

Micturition

Act of urinating, or expelling urine.

Mitochondria

Organelle that has a double membrane. The final stage of the aerobic respiration process takes place in mitochondria, where ATP is obtained by breaking down sugars and other substances.

Mitosis

Nuclear division in a cell that forms daughter nuclei identical to the parent.

Mucous Membrane

Covering of body cavities that communicate with the exterior (such as the nose). A mucous membrane contains numerous single-celled glands that secrete mucus.

Muscles

Organs composed of fibers capable of contracting.

Myocardium

Muscular part of the heart, between the pericardium and the endocardium.

Nucleic Acid

Molecule that carries genetic information about the cell. There are two types: DNA and RNA.

Nucleus

The part of the cell that contains the DNA with its genetic information.

Organ

Any part of the body that accomplishes a function.

Osmosis

Movement of a liquid through a selectively permeable membrane.

Papillae

Conical protuberances, usually sensory, formed on the skin or mucous membranes (especially the tongue) by the branching of nerves and blood vessels.

Pericardium

Pair of membranes that surround the heart.

Phagocytes

Cells found in blood and tissue. They capture bacteria or any other kind of noxious particles and "phagocytize," or "eat," them, absorbing them into their cytoplasm and later digesting them.

Phalanges

Bones of the fingers and toes. They extend to the metacarpal bones in the hand and the metatarsals in the foot. Starting from the metacarpals and the metatarsals, they are sequentially numbered: first, second, and third phalanges (of each finger or toe). The word "phalanges" commonly designates the first phalanges, or each of the jointed parts of the fingers or toes.

Physiology

Study of the functions of the organism.

Polymer

Macromolecule consisting of repeated structural units, called monomers.

Popliteus

Section of the leg opposed to, or behind, the knee.

Protein

Substance that makes up the cells. It is a biopolymer consisting of one or several chains o amino acids, fundamental for the constitution and functioning of living material, such as enzymes, hormones, and antibodies.

Ranine Artery

Artery that branches out toward the front of the tongue.

Respiration

The act and effect of inhaling air, primarily through the nose, to take in the substances that the body requires, such as oxygen, and after processing them exhaling unneeded substances, such as carbon dioxide.

Ribosome

Organelle located in the cytoplasm that governs the formation of proteins based on information provided by the nucleic acids.

Ribs

Long and curved bones. They originate at the back of the body at the spinal column and curve forward. They are called "true" if they end at the sternum and "false" if they remain floating without completely enclosing the rib cage.

Schwann Cells

Cells that produce myelin, a fatty insulating substance that prevents electrical signals from losing strength as they move away from the body of the neuron.

Semen

The spermatozoa and fluids produced in the male genital organs. It is often called sperm.

Sensation

Physiological process of receiving and recognizing stimuli produced by vision, hearing, smell, taste, touch, or the body's spatial orientation.

Sleep

State of repose characterized by inactivity or suspension of the senses and voluntary motion.

The cerebral activity called dreaming takes place during sleep.

Spinal

Relating to the spine.

Spinal Bulbar

Part of the cerebral trunk that goes from the annular protuberance to the cranium's occipital foramen.

Spine

The neuroskeletal axis that runs along the medial dorsal of the body and consists of a series of short bones called vertebrae, which are arranged in a column and jointed with each other.

Sternum

Bone of the anterior thorax, which joins the front of the ribs.

Striated Muscle

Muscle used for voluntary motion. Its muscle fibers show striations, or grooves.

Subclavian Arteries

Pair of arteries, one of which branches off from the brachiocephalic trunk (on the right side of the body) and the other from the aortic arc (on the left). They run toward the shoulder on each side and, after passing below the clavicle, become the axillary artery.

System

Complex of organs that participates in any of the principal functions of the body. A synonym of "apparatus."

Tarsal

The skeletal structure of the leg between the foot and the metatarsal. It consists of seven bones that constitute the posterior part of the foot.

Tissue

Group of identical cells that together accomplish a function.

Uterus

Hollow viscera of the female reproductive system. It is located inside a woman's pelvis. In the uterus, or womb, either menstrual fluid is produced or a fetus develops until it is born.

Veins

Blood vessels that bring blood from the entire body toward the heart.

Ventricles

Cavities of the heart that receive blood from their respective atrium (right or left) and pump it through the arteries.

Viscera

Organs located in the principal cavities of the body (such as the stomach or the liver within the abdominal cavity).

Vitamins

Organic substances present in food. The body ingests them to ensure the balance of various vital functions. There are different kinds of vitamins, designated with the letters A, B, C, etc.

Index

A

abducens nerve, 89
ABO blood system, 40
accessory nerve, 89
Achilles tendon, 31
actin filament, muscle fibers, 33
active transport, 13
Adam's apple, 46
adipose cell, 55
adrenal gland, 59, 61, 63
adrenocorticotropin hormone (ACTH), 62
afferent lymphatic vessel, 44
agranulocyte, 41
alveoli, 46, 48, 49
amino acid, protein synthesis, 55
amphiarthrose joint, 28
amygdala, 90, 91
anabolism, 55
anaphase (cell division), 15
anterior tibia, 31
anti-diuretic hormone (ADH), 62
antibody, 43
antioxidant, 14
aortic artery (aorta), 36, 39
aortic valve, 39
arm
    bones, 20
    circulatory system, 36-37
    joints, 28
    movement, 32, 33
    muscles, 30
artery, 36-37, 38
    kidneys, 58, 61
    knees, 29
    lungs, 49
astrocyte, 85
atlas bone, 26, 28
axial bone, 21
axis bone, 26, 28
axon, 32, 84

B

bacteria, 44, 45
basal joint, 28
Bernard, Claude, 60
bicep muscle, 30, 31
bile, 54
bladder, 58, 65
blood
    circulation, 16, 36-37
    components, 40-41
    glucose level regulation, 54, 55
    groups, 40
    oxygenation, 38, 40
    purification in kidneys, 60
bone
    cell types, 23
    cervical, 27
    development, 23
    fracture repair, 23
    function, 22
    lever function, 33
    skeleton, 20-21
    structure, 22-23
    types, 21
    See also joint
bone marrow, 22, 40, 43
bone shaft, 22, 23
Bowman capsule, 61
brain, 86-87
    astrocyte, 85
    communication, 79
    cranial nerves, 88-89
    cranium, 20
    dream states, 90, 91
    infant, 9
    limbic system, 91
    memory formation, 90, 91
    neurons, 8-9, 84-85
    olfactory receptors, 71
    taste center, 71
    weight, 9
brain cell, 8-9
Broca's area, 79, 87

bronchi, 47, 49
bronchial tree, 48

C

calcanum (calcaneus), 21, 27
calcium, 11, 22, 23
callus body, 87
capillary, 36, 37, 49
carbon, 11
cardiac muscle, 30, 31
    See also heart
carotid artery, 36
carpal bone, 20
cell
    division: See mitosis
    size, 6-7
    structure, 12-13
    transport mechanisms, 13
cell theory, 12
cellular membrane, 13
central nervous system, 82, 87
    brain: See brain
    spinal cord: See spinal cord
centriole, 13, 15
cerebellum (brain), 82, 86, 89, 90
cerebral cortex (brain) 9, 86-87, 88
cervical vertebra, 26
cervix (uterine), 67
cheekbone (zygomatic bone), 24-25
chemical element, contents of human body, 11
chlorine, 11
cholesterol, formation, 54
chromosome, 14
circulatory system, 16, 36-37
    See also artery; heart; vein
clavicle, 20
clitoris, 67
coccyx (tailbone), 21, 26, 27
cochlea, 76, 77
cochlear vestibular nerve, 89
colon, 57
color blindness, 75

communication, 78, 79
compact bone, 22
connective tissue, perineurium, 32
cornea, 74, 75
cortisol, 62
cranial nerve, 88-89
cranium, 20
   muscles, 33
   sinuses, 25
cubital nerve, 83
cubitum, 20
cytology, 12
cytoplasm, 12, 13
cytoskeleton, 12

D

Da Vinci, Leonardo, 20
deltoid muscle, 30
dendrite, 8, 84
diaphragm, 47, 48
diaphysis (bone), 22, 23
diarthrose joint, 28
diastolic: See heartbeat
dieting, muscle loss, 30
diffusion (cell), 13
digestive system, 17
   digestive process, 51
   intestine: See intestine
   liver, 54-55
   overview, 50
   pancreas, 54, 55
   peristalsis, 53
   spleen, 42, 55
   stomach, 51, 52-53
disease, 45
DNA, 13
dorsal vertebra, 26
dreaming, 90, 91

E

ear, 76, 77
   cranial nerves, 89
efferent lymphatic vessel, 45
ellipsoid joint, 28
endocrine system, 17, 62-63
   hypothalamus, 10, 86
   pancreas, 55
   See also hormone
endoplasmic reticulum, 12, 13
enzyme
   digestive process, 50
   pancreatic juice, 55
epididymis, 65
epiglottis, 46
epiphysis (bone), 23
equilibrium, 77
   cerebellum, 86
esophagus, 50, 52
estrogen, 62, 63
   menstrual cycle, 66
ethmoid bone, 24-25
excrement, 10, 51
eye, 74-75
   brain, 79, 87
   cranial nerves, 88, 89
   muscles, 30
   sleep, 91

F

face
   bones, 24-25
   cranial nerves, 88, 89
   muscles, 30, 31
   nonverbal communication, 79
facial nerve, 88
facilitated diffusion (cell), 13
fallopian tube, 66, 67
farsightedness (hyperopia), 75
fascicle, muscle fibers, 32

fat, storage, 55
female
   menopause, 67
   menstrual cycle, 66
   milk production, 62
   pelvis, 21
   reproductive system, 16, 67
   sexuality, 63
   skin, 73
   urinary system, 59
femur (thigh bone), 20, 21
   artery, 29
   vein, 37
fiber: See muscular fiber
fibula, 21, 29
finger, 20
   See also hand
flat bone, 21
follicle-stimulating hormone (FSH), 62, 66
fontanel, 24
food, 17
   digestive process, 50-51, 52, 56-57
   source of water, 10
foot
   articulation, 28
   bones, 27
   movement, 33
   muscles, 31
   nerves, 83
   toenails, 73
foramen magnum, cranium, 24
fracture, repair, 23
free radical, 14
frontal bone, 24-25
frontal lobe (brain), 87, 89
frontal muscle, 30
frowning, 31, 79
fusion, bones, 23

G

gallbladder, 54
gastrocnemius, 31

glomerulus, 58, 61
glosso-pharyngeal nerve, 89
gluteus maximus, 31
glycogen, storage, 54, 55
Golgi apparatus, 12
goose bump, 73
granulocyte, 41
gray matter (brain), 87
growth hormone (GH), 62
growth plate, 23
gustatory papilla, 70

H

hair, temperature regulation, 73
hand
    bones, 20, 27
    fingernails, 73
    joints, 28
    nerves, 83
    touch, 9
Havers conduit, bony tissue, 22
Hayflick, Leonard, 15
Hayflick limit (cell longevity), 15
head
    bone structure, 24-25
    circulatory system, 36
    movement, 33
    muscles, 30
hearing, 76, 77
heart, 36, 38-39
    cardiac muscle, 31
    valves, 39
heartbeat, 38
hematosis, 49
herniated disc, 26
hippocampus, 90, 91
homeostasis, 17, 58
Hooke, Robert, 12
hormone, 17, 62
    digestive process, 50
    menstrual cycle, 66
    See also endocrine system; pheromone

humerus, 20, 28
hydrogen, 11
hypermobility, 28
hyperopia (farsightedness), 75
hypoglossal nerve, 89
hypophysis: *See* pituitary gland
hypothalamus, 10, 86

I

ilium, 20
immune system, 43, 44
    spleen, 55
    See also lymphatic system; white blood cell
infant
    bones, 23
    brain development, 8-9
    cranium, 24
inferior maxillary, 20, 25
inferior vena cava, 36, 59
insulin, 11, 55
interphase (cell division), 14
intestinal mucosa, 44
intestine, 51, 56-57
    duodenum, 52, 54
iodine, 11
iris, 74
iron, 11
irregular bone, 21

J

jaw bone, 20
joint, 28-29
    lever function, 33
    noise, 29
jugular vein, 36

K

kidney, 58, 59, 60-61
    Bowman capsule, 61
    nephrons, 61
    renal vein, 36
kissing, hormone stimulation, 63
knee
    articulation, 28
    joint, 29
kneecap (patella), 21, 29

L

lachrymal bone, 24-25
lachrymal gland, 44
larynx, 46, 47
leg
    bones, 21
    circulatory system, 36-37
    knee: *See* knee
    muscles, 31
    nerves, 83
lens (eye), 74
Leonardo da Vinci, 20
leukocyte, 41
ligament, knee, 29
limbic system, 91
liver, 54-55
long bone, 21
lumbar vertebra, 27
lung, 47, 48-49
    circulatory system, 36, 38
luteinizing hormone (LH), 62, 63, 66
lymphatic system, 16, 42-43
    lymph nodes, 44-45
    lymphocytes, 45
lysosome, 12

M

macrophage, 45-46
magnesium, 11
male
  hormones, 62
  pelvis, 21
  reproductive system, 17, 64-65
  skin, 73
  urinary system, 59
master gland: See pituitary gland
melanocyte-stimulating hormone (MSH), 62
memory formation, 90, 91
men: See male
menarche, 67
meninges, 86, 87
meniscus, 29
menopause, 67
menstrual cycle, 66
metabolism, 55
metacarpal bone, 20
metaphase (cell division), 14
metatarsal bone, 21
milk, production, 62
mitochondria, 13
mitosis, 6-7, 12, 14-15
mitral valve, 39
mouth
  digestive function, 50, 51
  sound production, 78
  swallowing, 52
mucous secretion, 44
muscle
  function: See muscular fiber
  movement, 30, 87
  types, 31
muscular fiber, 32-33
  glycogen storage, 55
muscular system, 17, 30-31
musculoskeletal system, 18-19, 30
  See also muscular system; skeletal system
myelin sheath, 84
  oligodendrocytes, 85
myofibril, muscle fibers, 33

myopia (nearsightedness), 75
myosin filament, muscle fibers, 33

N

nails, 73
nasal concha, 24-25
nasal fossa,
  olfactory nerve, 71
  sensations, 9
nearsightedness (myopia), 75
neck, bones, 28
nephron, 60, 61
nervous system, 16, 82-83
  brain: See brain
  neuron: See neuron
  pain signals, 83
  spinal column, 20, 26-27
  spinal cord, 87
neuromuscular union, 85
neuron, 8-9, 84-85, 86
  dendrites, 8, 84
  microscope photograph, 80-81
neurotransmitter, 9, 85
nitrogen, 11
nonverbal communication, 78, 79
nose
  bones, 24-25
  cranial nerves, 88, 89
  nasal fossa, 9, 71
  olfactory cells, 70
  sound production, 78
NREM (non-rapid eye movement) sleep, 91
nucleole, 13
nucleus, 12, 13

O

oblique muscle, 30
occipital bone, 20, 24-25
occipital lobe (brain), 86

occipital muscle, 30
oculomotor nerve, 89
olfactory cell, 70
olfactory nerve, 71, 89
oligodendrocyte, 85
optic nerve, 88
orbicular muscle, 30
organ of Corti, 76
osteoblast, 23
osteoclast, 23
ovary, 66, 67
ovulation, 66
ovum, 66, 67
oxygen, 11, 40
oxytocin, 62, 63

P

pain signal, 83
palatine, 24-25
pancreas, 11, 54, 55, 63
parietal bone, 24
patella (kneecap), 21, 29
pathogen, types, 45
pectoralis major, 30
pedis, 31
pelvis, 20, 67
  joint, 21
penis, 59, 64, 65
periosteum, 22, 23
peripheral nervous system, 82, 88-89
peristalsis, digestive system, 51, 53
peroxisome (organelle), 13
perspiration: See sweat; sweat gland
Peyer's patch, 42
phalange, 20, 21
pharynx, 47, 50
pheromone, 63
phosphorus, 11
photosensitive cell, 75
pituitary gland, hormones, 62, 63
plane, 28
plasma, 41

plasma membrane: *See* cellular membrane
platelet, 41
popliteal artery, 29
pore (cell), 13
potassium (K), 11
pregnancy, 66, 67
progesterone, menstrual cycle, 66
prolactin, 62
prophase (cell division), 14
prostate gland, 65
protein, 11
    metabolism, 12, 54
    synthesis, 55
protozoa, pathogens, 45
pulmonary artery, 48
pulmonary valve, 39
pylorus, 52

Q-R

quadriceps, 31
radius, 20, 28
Ranvier's node, 84
rapid eye movement (REM) sleep, 91
rectus abdominis, 30
red blood cell, 40
REM sleep, 91
renal vein, 36
reproductive system
    female, 16, 66-67
    hormones, 62
    male, 17, 64-65
respiration, 9, 46
    process, 46-47, 48
respiratory system, 17, 46-47
    See also lung
retina, 74, 75
Rh factor, 40
rib cage, 20, 26
ribosome, 12
rough endoplasmic reticulum, 12

S

sacroiliac joint, 21
sacrum, 20, 26, 27
salivary gland, 44, 70
salt: *See* sodium
sarcomere, muscle fibers, 33
Schleiden, Mathias, 12
Schwann, Theodor, 12
Schwann cell, 84
sciatic nerve, 83
sclera, 75
sebaceous gland, 44, 73
sensation: *See* hearing; smell; taste; touch;
    vision
septum, 39
sesamoid bone, 21
sexual attraction, 63
short bone, 21
shoulder, articulation, 28
sight, 74-75
sinus cavity, 25
skeletal system (skeleton), 16
    structure, 20-21
    See also joint; musculoskeletal system
skin, 9, 44, 72-73, 87
    cellular division, 14
    melanocyte production, 62
    wound healing, 45
sleep, 91
smell, 70, 71, 90
smooth endoplasmic reticulum, 13
smooth muscle, 30, 31
sodium, 11
speech, 78, 87
speech recognition technology, 24
spermatozoa, 64
sphenoid bone, 24-25
spheroid, 28
spinal column, 20, 26-27
spinal cord, 26, 82, 87, 88
spinal medulla, 87
spinal nerve, 88
spleen, 42, 43, 55

splenius muscle, 30
spongy bone, 22
Starling, Ernest, 62
sternocleidomastoid muscle, 30
sternum, 20, 26
stomach, 51, 52-53
striated muscle, 17, 30, 31
subclavian vein, 42
sugar, regulation in blood, 11
sulfur, 11
superior maxillary, 24-25
superior vena cava, 36, 39
swallowing, 52
sweat, 10, 73
sweat gland, 44
synapse, 8, 85
synaptic node, 84
synarthrose joint, 28
systole: *See* heartbeat

T

T cell, 45
    See also lymphatic system
tailbone (coccyx), 21, 26, 27
Takagi, Kenji, 29
tarsal bone, 21
taste, 70, 71
    types, 9
technology, speech recognition, 24
teeth, structure, 50
telophase (cell division), 15
temperature regulation, 73
temporal artery, 36
temporal bone, 24-25
temporal lobe (brain), 86, 89, 90
temporal vein, 36
tendinous cord, 39
testicle, 64, 65
testosterone, 62, 63, 65
thalamus, 86
thigh bone: *See* femur
thirst, control, 10

thoracic vertebra, 26
thumb, joints, 28
thymus, 42, 43
thyroid-stimulating hormone (TSH), 62
tibia, 21, 29
toe, nails, 73
tongue
    functions, 50, 51
    gustatory papillae, 70, 71
    nervous system, 88
    sensations, 9
    sound production, 78
tonsils, 42
touch, 9, 72-73
trachea, 46, 47, 49
transport mechanism (cell), 13
trapezium muscle, 30
tricep muscle, 30
tricuspid valve, 39
trigeminal nerve, 71, 88
trochlear nerve, 89

valve
    heart, 39
    lymphatic system, 45
vein, 36-37
    inferior vena cava, 36, 59
    kidneys, 58, 61
    lymphatic system, 42
    superior vena cava, 36, 39
vertebral column: See spinal column
vesicle, 13
villi (intestine), 57
virus, pathogens, 45
vision, 74-75, 87
vocal cord, 46, 78
    See also speech
vomer (bone), 24-25
vulva, 66

U

ureter, 58, 59
urethra, 58
urinary system, 17, 58-59
    gender differences, 59
    kidneys, 60-61
urine, 10, 58, 59, 64
    Bowman capsule, 61
    production, 60
uterus, 66, 67

V

vacuole, 13
vagina, 66, 67
    bacteria, 44
vagus nerve, 82, 89

W-Z

water
    fluid exchange, 10, 59
    intake, 10
    intestines, 56
Wernicke's area (brain), 79
white blood cell, 41, 45
white matter (brain), 87
women: See female
wound healing, 45
Z band, muscle fibers, 33
zygomatic bone (cheekbone), 24-25